'GET WISDOM, GET INSIGHT'

'GET WISDOM, GET INSIGHT'

An Introduction to Israel's Wisdom Literature

Katharine Dell

DARTON·LONGMAN+TODD

First published in 2000 by
Darton, Longman and Todd Ltd
1 Spencer Court
140–142 Wandsworth High Street
London sw18 4jj

ISBN 0–232–52266–9

A catalogue record for this book is available from the British Library.

Designed by Sandie Boccacci
Phototypeset in 8.75/13.75pt Walbaum
by Intype London Ltd
Printed and bound in Great Britain
by Page Bros, Norwich, Norfolk

To my parents, Robert and Molly Dell

'Hear, my child, your father's instruction, and do not reject your mother's teaching; for they are a fair garland for your head, and pendants for your neck.' (Proverbs 1:8–9)

CONTENTS

ABBREVIATIONS

BETL	Bibliotheca Ephemeridum Theologicarum Lovaniensium
BZAW	Beihefte zur Zeitschrift für die alttestamentliche Wissenschaft
CBQ	*Catholic Biblical Quarterly*
CRINT	Compendia Rerum Iudaicarum ad Novum Testamentum
DSD	*Dead Sea Discoveries*
HUCA	Hebrew Union College Annual
JAOS	*Journal of the American Oriental Society*
JBL	*Journal of Biblical Literature*
JQR	*Jewish Quarterly Review*
JQR NS	*Jewish Quarterly Review New Series*
JSOP	*Journal for the Study of the Pseudepigrapha*
JSOT	*Journal for the Study of the Old Testament*
JSOTS	Journal for the Study of the Old Testament Supplement Series
JSS	*Journal of Semitic Studies*
JTS NS	*Journal of Theological Studies* New Series
OBO	Orbis Biblicus et Orientalis
PTMS	Pittsburgh Theological Monograph Series
RB	*Revue Biblique*
SBL	Society of Biblical Literature
SBL MS	Society of Biblical Literature Monograph Series
SBS	Stuttgarter Bibelstudien
SBT	Studies in Biblical Theology
SJT	*Scottish Journal of Theology*
SUNT	Studien zur Umwelt des Neuen Testaments
SVT	Supplements to Vetus Testamentum
VT	*Vetus Testamentum*
WMANT	Wissenschaftliche Monographieren zum Alten und Neuen Testament
WUNT	Wissenschaftliche Untersuchungen zum Neuen Testament
ZAW	*Zeitschrift für die alttestamentliche Wissenschaft*

PREFACE

This book has taken shape over a number of years, some of the ideas first emerging as a result of my doctoral work and others the result of teaching the Old Testament for the last ten years, six of them at Ripon College, Cuddesdon and four in the University of Cambridge. I have appreciated enormously the opportunity to lecture on wisdom in various contexts and have learnt much from discussions over weekly essays with students from both institutions for which I am grateful. My particular thanks go to Professor John Emerton who kindly read and commented upon this manuscript and to Dr Douglas Hamilton who has patiently read material foreign to his own subject in the quest for typographical and grammatical errors. I would also like to thank my parents for their help in finalising this manuscript and for always giving me freely and generously of their wisdom and insight. It is with love and gratitude that I dedicate this book to them. I should also like to mention one of my cats, Keziah, who sat quietly on my lap for much of the writing of this book!

Cambridge,
June 1999

1: INTRODUCTORY QUESTIONS OF DEFINITION, SCOPE AND INFLUENCE

The beginning of wisdom is this: Get wisdom, and whatever else you get, get insight. (Prov. 4:7)

As this proverb exhorts, wisdom is an attribute that we should all strive to acquire. Wisdom here is paired with insight or understanding, itself a prerequisite for wisdom – for how can one be wise if one does not understand what one is talking about? The *Oxford English Dictionary* describes wisdom as a combination of knowledge and experience. For wisdom is not just about learning from books or second-hand from parents or friends, it is also about experiencing for ourselves. However, every experience needs to be put into a context of teachings from the experience of others so that it can be understood in a scheme of things. This is where the wisdom books of the Old Testament come in. They represent the teaching of the wise men of ancient Israel: their maxims distilled from the experiences of many generations, their advice to the young seeking to understand and grow in maturity, their example tales and warnings.

An important distinction needs to be made between 'wisdom' as an attribute that is God-given and that we should all strive to 'Get'; and wisdom as denoting a genre of material contained in the Bible and other books which have the nature of specialist wisdom writings from the past. The Hebrew term for wisdom – *ḥokmāh* – covers a wide range of attributes that constitute wisdom in particular contexts. It includes the skill needed to win a war or complete a technical enterprise; the cleverness and shrewdness required in government or administration; the hidden secrets and knowledge of prophets or magicians; the prudence required to deal with difficult situations; the ability to make ethical or religious decisions, and ultimately the ability to discern God as the one who created the world through wisdom and who is the fount of all knowledge and understanding. It is a rich and multifaceted term covering both the human quest for wisdom and the divine origin of wisdom.

'Wisdom' as a description of a genre of material is a well-known usage of the term in scholarly circles to explain a phenomenon that extends throughout the world, in that the collection of wisdom sayings is a human activity common to all cultures. We have sayings from Africa and China, we have sayings of the Vikings, and we have wisdom from cultures older than the Bible, from ancient Sumer, Egypt and Mesopotamia in particular. Any saying that belongs in general terms to this wisdom genre has a claim to be included in a consideration of the universal phenomenon of wisdom. However, in biblical studies the term has been narrowed to describe the wisdom phenomenon in Israel and in surrounding cultures in the ancient Near East. The writings that contain most of the wisdom of the Old Testament are generally termed the 'wisdom literature' and this is a well-known corpus of material. The influence of wisdom and its genres, however, can be found amongst a much wider spread of material within the Old Testament itself, as well as outside.

The wisdom literature of the Old Testament has often been felt to be a strange companion to the rest of the Old Testament because it does not concern itself with the covenant or the saving history of Israel. Rather, like its international counterparts, it is concerned with defining what constitutes wisdom, advising on how to get it and how to behave, it is concerned with human understanding of life and its structures and orders, and it is ultimately concerned with the God-givenness of the enterprise. Its God is primarily the creator and orderer of the universe, and its view of humanity is one that sees human beings as needing to seek understanding for themselves. It is concerned with the human condition and with relationships between individuals, between human beings and the world around them, and between human beings and God. It has sometimes been seen as the 'foreign element' in Israelite thought because it seems to have sprung largely from contact with the wisdom of other nations rather than from within Israelite tradition itself. However, as we shall see, despite shared characteristics with ancient Near Eastern wisdom, Israelite wisdom has its own character and its own place in a distinctively Israelite realm of ideas.

Having noted the separate identity and distinctiveness of the wisdom literature we might also note how in fact wisdom influence can be found throughout the Old Testament, in the Pentateuch, in the Prophets and in the Psalms in particular. Furthermore, writings belonging to the wisdom genre are not restricted to the Old Testament books of Proverbs, Job and Ecclesiastes; rather, they extend into the Apocrypha, with the books of Ben Sira and the Wisdom of Solomon in particular. These Apocryphal works begin to redress the balance of the absence of other areas of Israel's life in biblical wisdom literature, in the mention of the Torah, salvation history, prophecy and prayer within their pages. Writings influenced by wisdom extend further into the Pseudepigrapha, New Testament and other early Jewish and Christian writings, as well as including exciting new material amongst the Qumran writings found by the shores of the Dead Sea.

Wisdom literature has never been high on the agenda of worshipping communities, intellectuals or scholars. In Jewish circles, with emphasis being placed most highly on the Torah, followed by the prophets, wisdom as part of the writings section of the Hebrew Bible was of lesser concern. Similarly for Christians, with the prophets at the centre of concern (focusing on the fulfilment of ancient prophecy in the person and life, death and resurrection of Jesus Christ) and the law in second place, the writings were marginalised, except within worshipping communities where the psalms also had pride of place. Wisdom however was rather on the sidelines, and so it was in biblical scholarship of only fifty years ago where it was felt to have a marginal place because of its lack of mention of the big themes of the Old Testament – Yahweh's self-revelation in the Exodus, the promises to David and the election of Israel as a covenant people. Any literature that did not concern itself with the heartland of the Old Testament could not, it was thought, be of central concern.

Biblical scholarship of the last forty years has, however, been moving in the direction of appreciating the wisdom literature afresh. Recognition of the widespread influence of wisdom on other parts of the Old Testament is part of this interest, although wisdom has been put on the agenda also for its own sake. This interest may have something to do with appreciation of plurality in the modern age and the recognition that insight comes from many quarters, not just from one central point. The wisdom literature has come into its own in the recognition that it is an alternative and in many ways complementary mode of revelation in the Bible which speaks to us today in a world where belief in God as creator is as important as belief in God as redeemer and in a century where confidence in the enormity of human potential and achievement runs high.

Questions of definition

The books that are widely considered to be wisdom books in the Old Testament are, of course, Proverbs, Job and Ecclesiastes or Qoheleth, and in the Apocrypha, Ecclesiasticus or Ben Sira and the Wisdom of Solomon (see Chapters 2, 3, 4, 8, 9). When we classify these books as wisdom we need to be careful in our definitions of terms. As I have mentioned, we need to distinguish between wisdom as an attribute and wisdom as a genre. However, we also need to go on to make a further distinction between wisdom as a description of the genre of material containing certain known forms, an easily characterisable content and practised in a suitable context, and 'wisdom literature' which is a description of this group of books that we want to designate as containing wisdom. The two are not one and the same because we can talk of wisdom as a genre that we may find in the prophets whilst at the same time knowing that no one – not even the keenest promoter of wisdom – would designate any of the prophetic books as 'wisdom literature'. We might instead use the term 'wisdom influence' in such cases. We would want to designate as wisdom literature only those books which contain to a high degree the material we would define as wisdom. It is almost universally agreed that these five books are to be defined as wisdom literature, but we will need to test this afresh for ourselves on grounds of form, content and context. A recent challenge to this kind of form-critical approach has been voiced by J. J. Collins, who argues that the context of 'instruction' is more definitive of what constitutes wisdom literature than a study of literary forms and content or a study of 'worldview', as in the approach of other scholars. He writes: 'The coherence of wisdom literature, however, lies in its use as instructional material rather than in literary form, strictly defined' (1997a, p. 281). While I would condone other methods of defining the limits of the wisdom literature, I have a certain unease with all the emphasis being put on context, as I have with all the weight being put on the theological outlook of the wisdom literature. I would contend that a study of form, content and context is a valid method, and that only when we have these three aspects in large measure can a book be strictly defined as 'wisdom literature'.

So first we need to define and characterise wisdom, and what better starting place is there than the book of Proverbs, a book universally acknowledged as the supreme example of traditional Israelite wisdom? From this starting point, we can go on to evaluate material we might want to consider as wisdom. If a book seems to contain to a large extent the same kinds of form and content and possible context that we have found in Proverbs, we might well want to classify that book as 'wisdom literature'. If however we find only isolated examples of wisdom genres amongst other material, we might suggest wisdom influence but not wish to consider the book as generically a wisdom book. The genre of wisdom itself is seen to be made up of diverse elements – are we right to characterise it in this way using the book of Proverbs? It is clear that the proverb is the basic form of all wisdom and in that sense is at the heart of the enterprise, and this book contains the earliest wisdom material found in the wisdom corpus (notably in Proverbs 10:1—22:16 which is made up of a miscellany of sayings which may well have had an oral origin).

However, whilst the book of Proverbs is a good place to begin, we need to exercise caution, as with any starting point, because we have to allow for development over time. So while for the generations that cited the proverbs, and for those who wrote them down, confidence in the benefits of acquiring wisdom may have been high, for a later generation the quest may have had a less optimistic flavour, as we in fact find when we arrive at another well-established work of the wisdom literature, Ecclesiastes. Here we are into a much more negative evaluation of the wisdom quest and there are maxims on the futility of the enterprise. New forms naturally spring up to express new concerns, while some forms will develop a more sophisticated structure. The content may contain contradictions or become more theological, and the context may well change. We can in fact chart a change in the wisdom world-view away from a more optimistic evaluation of the successful results of following the wisdom path, towards a realisation that life does not always work out in the way expected and that wisdom has its limitations. The material also seems to have developed in the direction of being more overtly theological (although scholars continue to debate the question of how theological Proverbs itself is, as we shall see). However, scholars are divided in their opinion as to which developments and changes took place and precisely when. We need to chart the kinds of developments that make sense, using as our starting point the character of the material in Proverbs. This point about development leads to uncertainty as to what wisdom really is and what material to include as wisdom literature, and means that the attempt to define both is made more complex.

Many scholars have tried to find a phrase or sentence that sums wisdom up in a nutshell, but wisdom is so diverse as a phenomenon that to pin it down in this way leads to problems. Definitions are usually too broad and fail to do justice to the divine aspect of the wisdom enterprise. So the description of wisdom as 'non-revelatory speech' (cited by Crenshaw, 1974), while it conveys the essence of wisdom as coming from the human side, is too broad in that any part of the Old Testament which takes its starting point from human experience rather than divine revelation could be included. It also excludes the divine element of the wisdom enterprise, in that God is at the limits of the quest and a presupposition of the whole wisdom enterprise. Tension between the human and divine is at the centre of an understanding of wisdom, and the wisdom enterprise is to be characterised by this tension between the two emphases. The starting point of wisdom is clearly in the human attempt to make life comprehensible and manageable, to seek to understand its nature and its patterns. In that sense, wisdom is non-revelatory and experiential. Yet there is a divine aspect that is ever present, an order that can be known, a God at the limits of knowledge and the search for experiential wisdom. This tension can be found in Proverbs 8 in the figure of wisdom who is closely associated with the divine, 'The Lord created me at the beginning of his work' (Prov. 8:22a); and who calls on humans to follow the path of tried and tested experiential wisdom, 'And now, my children, listen to me: happy are those who keep my ways' (Prov. 8:32).

Another suggested definition of wisdom is 'the ability to cope' (Kenworthy, 1974) which has a pithiness that is attractive but is again anthropocentric and broad as a definition. There is also von Rad's definition of 'practical knowledge of the laws of life and of the world, based on experience' ([1958–61] 1962a, p. 418) which is also anthropocentric and relates to his idea of wisdom as essentially an 'act-consequence relationship' whereby every action has a consequence that can be known as a result of inherited experience. Again the divine element is lacking. R. N. Whybray (1974) labels wisdom as a style of intellectual and spiritual quest, putting his emphasis on the intellectual aspect of being 'wise'. On this definition wisdom is seen as an intellectual movement and the religious dimension of wisdom also comes across, but perhaps to the detriment of the practical aspects. It is also broad in its scope, but then all definitions tend in this direction. J. L. McKenzie (1967) argues that wisdom was a living tradition, a way of thought and speech, and is against the idea of confining it to particular genres or contexts. He finds the genre category 'wisdom literature' too narrow. The question of context is also raised: we may wish to abandon the idea of a particular group of sages along with the idea of a particular literary corpus, but should perhaps exercise caution before doing so. The 'wisdom literature' may well have been written down by specialists, but the wisdom enterprise is clearly broader than this.

The advantage then of distinguishing between 'wisdom literature' as a narrower description and 'wisdom' as a broader one is that it allows us to explore beyond the accepted boundaries of wisdom so that we are not constrained by definitions, while still allowing us to retain the distinctiveness of those books that show the forms, content and context in such large measure that they are wisdom *par excellence*. We therefore need to be careful to confine to the wisdom literature parts of the Bible which not only show the influence of an intellectual and spiritual quest or a particular approach to 'reality' (von Rad, [1970] 1972), but also employ the distinctive forms of wisdom and are concerned with particular types of questions which characterise a wisdom content and which may belong to a similar context as other wisdom books – in other words, those that contain wisdom genres in large measure. Yet, at the same time, we need to be able to explore a wider range of texts in order to recognise the widespread influence of the genre. So, we need to bear this discussion of terms in mind as we go on to look at the wisdom literature and at the wisdom elements in the Bible.

Questions of scope and influence

The question of which texts to include as wisdom follows on naturally from that of definition. The Song of Songs has sometimes been included on the basis of parallels with Egyptian love poems and on the grounds of Solomonic attribution (Ranston, 1930). However, Solomonic attribution is more likely to be a means of giving authority to later texts. The prime example of this is Ecclesiastes, a book most likely to belong to the post-exilic age so that the hints that the 'son of David' (Eccl. 1:1, 12) was involved in its production are generally taken as either a rather strained attempt to give the book authority (by the author or by subsequent redactors linking it with the 'father' of wisdom, Solomon) or the simple use of a famous king as a literary device, in the manner of a royal testament (see Chapter 4). In fact whilst Solomon was famed for his wisdom – and we read in 1 Kings 10 of his responding to 'hard questions' posed by the Queen of Sheba, none of which were too difficult for him – most of the wisdom books are dated later than his reign. He may have had some input into the formulation of some proverbs, but it is likely that much of the proverbial material was simply gathered together under his name rather than originating with him. He is described in 1 Kings 4:33: 'He spoke of trees, from the cedar that is in Lebanon to the hyssop that grows out of the wall; he spoke also of beasts, and of birds, and of reptiles, and of fish.' In Jewish tradition, rather as everything to do with the law is ascribed to Moses and all psalms are ascribed to David, so to Solomon is accorded all wisdom. All the so-called wisdom books in the Old Testament are attributed to Solomon, except Job. We have to ask, however, how authentic these attributions are. They may well have been added to the collections at a fairly late stage in order to give an authoritative voice to the material. Alternatively, some of them may have some historical connection to Solomon, but, like the psalms in relation to David, once he was connected with one, he was connected with all. Interestingly Solomon's kind of wisdom is a very primitive, nature wisdom of which we find relatively little in the book of Proverbs. We find some similes and metaphors using plants and animals to illuminate human behaviour, such as the metaphor of the thorns: 'The way of the lazy. is overgrown with thorns, but the path of the upright is a level highway' (Prov. 15:19). We also find numerical proverbs as in Proverbs 30: 'Under three things the earth trembles; under four it cannot bear up' (vv. 21–2), but, in general, Solomon does not really seem to characterise what we actually have in the main bulk of the wisdom literature. Maybe then we should not use these attributions as too serious a criterion when we come to classify the wisdom books.

A whole range of other texts have a claim to be included as wisdom literature. There is the group of psalms designated 'wisdom psalms' (see Chapter 5) and there are sections of longer texts which arguably share the wisdom world-view, notably narratives such as the Joseph story and Succession Narrative (see Chapter 6). These are put into this category of wisdom because they reveal a particular interest in human relationships and interactions, rather than having their starting point, as so many Old Testament narratives do, in divine revelation. Thus the Joseph story of Genesis was included by G. von Rad ([1953] 1966c), the figure of Joseph being seen as the epitome of the successful administrator, which in Egyptian circles would place him amongst the wise and which may in Israel form part of the context of wisdom. The Succession Narrative of 2 Samuel 9—20 and 1 Kings 1—2 was included by R. N. Whybray (1968), a narrative about the courtly machinations that accompanied the way to the succession to the throne, told in very human-centred terms with God on the fringes. Both these inclusions in the wisdom category rely on the idea of a court context, which is a matter of debate among recent scholars. Both also assume that the human quest is what lies at the heart of a characterisation of wisdom. It may be more appropriate to classify these narratives as containing wisdom influence rather than including them in our corpus of wisdom literature proper – we need to consider the wisdom psalms too in relation to this distinction. It is certainly more applicable to speak of wisdom influence when noting traditional wisdom sayings within larger texts, for example 1 Samuel 16:7; 24:13 (Fontaine, 1982), and when noting wisdom influence on the prophetic books. No one would wish to categorise any of the prophetic books as wisdom literature; rather, it is a matter of wisdom's influence, and thus begs the question of context. Was wisdom simply a widespread phenomenon that started to appear within various different genres of material? This leads us to think of wisdom influence in Deuteronomy, which no one would deny is a law book, but which shows a broad ethical and humanitarian concern easily connected with the wisdom enterprise (Weinfeld, 1972). Was it a mark of being educated, taught perhaps in schools as a basic training for sages, prophets and priests? Was it therefore a formative influence on the thought of prophets? Or was it an editorial activity pursued by those who put the texts together as literary units, a final-stage phenomenon rather than an early influence on texts? These questions will be explored in Chapter 6.

Questions of context

Problems over the limits of the wisdom literature and the extent of wisdom influence lead to these questions of context. The wisdom enterprise clearly has its own distinctive character and this has led many to assume that a separate group of sages existed, quite distinct from other groups such as prophets and priests, even though existing alongside them. Jeremiah 18:18 is often used as evidence of a particular social group 'the wise' (ḥākām): 'For instruction shall not perish from the priest, nor counsel from the wise, nor the word from the prophet' (see the discussion in Whybray, 1974). However, the large extent of wisdom influence on other parts of the Old Testament has led to the suggestion of schools of wisdom to educate all who went into higher positions in the state. On this school model, wisdom would represent a particular training with a special role in relation to king and court and to the processes of administration and diplomacy, much on an Egyptian model. It would have influenced the written form of court narratives. It would not be confined to 'the wise', rather all men of influence would have gone through training in its arts.

An alternative to this, however, is to see wisdom as a wider thought-world, not confined to intellectuals and therefore not restricted to a school context. Wisdom could be seen as basic education undertaken in families, in the home or in local schools, and hence being a major formative influence on all kinds of oral transmission, influencing other areas of Israelite life such as its worship and the development of its ethics and laws. At the other end of the spectrum is the idea that the enterprise is primarily a literary one, an influence on writing rather than speaking. Thus wisdom could be regarded as a formative literary influence at, say, the time of the monarchy or as a later literary redaction of earlier material primarily in the post-exilic period. If the latter is correct, redactors from wisdom circles would have edited a wide range of works, pulling them into a more literary framework, and hence the discovery of wisdom forms and ideas in other parts of the Old Testament would hardly be surprising. There is also the point that wisdom itself was starting to diversify in the post-exilic period, leading Whybray (1974) to argue for the existence of an ongoing intellectual tradition in Israel rather than for a distinct group of sages. Thus the attempt to distinguish wisdom from other genres becomes even more complex. These are questions which have been the subject of much debate in recent scholarship and which I shall go on to discuss in the next chapter.

One aspect of the study of wisdom is that it is not a distinctively Israelite exercise. The wisdom quest is much older and more universal than the texts of the Old Testament indicate. The exact nature of the influence of ancient Near Eastern wisdom upon the formulation of Israelite wisdom is a question that has excited much debate. Was there direct borrowing? Or are parallels simply likely developments within cultures with similar world-views? Furthermore, the context of Israelite wisdom has often been reconstructed on the basis of what we know of the structures in nation states, such as Egypt, with its developed administration systems and class of those with time for leisure and intellectual pursuits. Are we right to extrapolate in this way or should we be seeking different models for a distinctively Israelite wisdom enterprise? In the last few decades the substantial importance of archaeological finds from these cultures for biblical studies has emerged and so we need to assign the ancient Near East its rightful place in our discussion. Yet, we might call for caution in drawing parallels too quickly. We need perhaps to have in mind first the forms and structures of the Israelite material before we try to shape it into the concerns of extra-biblical material in order to avoid distortion of its nature and its likely contexts.

Questions of definition, scope and influence should therefore be at the heart of our approach to the wisdom material. We need to determine the limits of the category of wisdom literature and this will involve some discussion of works that have been claimed to be part of that corpus outside the five mainstream wisdom books. It is also necessary for us to be clear about the criteria for discovering wisdom influence in texts so that the definition of wisdom does not itself become so broad as to be meaningless. There are those scholars who wish to cast the wisdom net widely (Morgan, 1981) and those who prefer to narrow its scope (Crenshaw, 1982). It is our task to pick our way through the various scholarly suggestions and evaluate them, looking first at the main biblical wisdom books, then at the broader range of suggestions for wisdom influence and at the ancient Near East, ending with an evaluation of the later wisdom books as they broaden out in their concerns and a consideration of fresh contexts for wisdom at Qumran and in the New Testament.

It is thus the purpose of this book to look at what wisdom is and who wrote it; at what should be included as wisdom literature in the Old Testament, and at the diversity of material that makes up wisdom in Israel. I shall use categories of form, content and context as criteria for evaluating the material. I shall begin with chapters on the main Old Testament wisdom books, Proverbs, Job and Qoheleth or Ecclesiastes. I shall then consider the so-called 'wisdom psalms', and then move on to the wider question of wisdom's influence in the Old Testament. I shall then consider wisdom's place in the ancient Near East as a whole as the background to the Israelite context. I shall consider the two major wisdom works in the Apocrypha, the book of Ecclesiasticus or Ben Sira and the Wisdom of Solomon in the chapters that follow, also looking at other contenders for the wisdom category among apocryphal and pseudepigraphical works. Then the new wisdom material from Qumran will be charted, followed by a survey of the wisdom influence on the sayings of Jesus in the New Testament. I shall end with some concluding reflections on wisdom's place, significance and legacy. My purpose is to introduce the reader to wisdom and its concepts but through the lens of scholarly concerns. It will be seen that the last decade has brought forth some interesting new developments in wisdom scholarship to which I will draw particular attention in this book.

2: PROVERBS

How much better to get wisdom than gold! To get under-
standing is to be chosen rather than silver. (Prov. 16:16)

Our best starting point in any consideration of the
wisdom material is the book of Proverbs, which contains some of the oldest wisdom maxims collected by the sages of
Israel. No one would deny that Proverbs contains wisdom genres and
is to be classified as wisdom literature. It is therefore a good point
to start when trying to define wisdom. Whybray writes in his commentary on Proverbs, 'To call Proverbs a book of wisdom is fully
justified. The word "wisdom" (*ḥokmāh* in Hebrew) occurs thirty-
nine times and the adjective "wise" (*ḥākām*) forty-seven times in
these thirty-one chapters' (1994c, p. 3). Furthermore, the basic form
of wisdom is the proverb of which the book chiefly consists. If we
characterise the forms, content and context so far as it can be known
of the book of Proverbs and then compare other books to it, we shall
be well on the way to defining the nature of wisdom as a genre and
will have a starting point from which to clarify the extent of the
wisdom literature. This is the approach to be taken in this book. The
book of Proverbs is made up of a number of collections, the oldest
of which is Proverbs 10:1—22:16, which consists of mainly proverbial
sayings. Proverbs 22:17—24:22 is generally dated fairly early and
marked off as a separate section on the grounds of similarity with
the Egyptian Instruction of Amenemope. Other collections are Proverbs 25—9, described as having been copied by the 'men of
Hezekiah' (Prov. 25:1), a seventh-century king of Israel, and Proverbs
30 and 31 which are separate shorter pieces, each with its own
attribution. Finally, there is Proverbs 1—9, which is often considered
the latest part of the book but which may well contain earlier
material. This is the more theologically developed part and may have
been placed at the beginning of the final book as a kind of preface
to the whole.

Form

The prime form in the book of Proverbs is, unsurprisingly, the proverb – a single or double-line sentence, its content usually characterised by comments about human relationships in everyday life and by analogies between nature and human experience in an attempt not only to further understanding but also to master life by noting regular patterns. For example, 'Like clouds and wind without rain is one who boasts of a gift never given' (Prov. 25:14). The repetition of experience led to the establishment of a principle so that patterns could be found that represented truth, not cold facts but truths based on repeated observation, truths about human beings in relationship with each other and with the natural world around them. Different areas of life were closely examined and patterns were found which allowed a picture of the world gradually to emerge within which individuals could make sense of their own lives.

There is a variety of different forms in which we find the basic proverb. Sometimes proverbs consist simply of statements of fact with no comparative element, for example, Proverbs 20:14: ' "Bad, bad," says the buyer, then goes away and boasts.' There are proverbs in which the consequence of an action is pointed out in exhortatory tone: 'My child, fear the Lord and the king, and do not disobey either of them; for disaster comes from them suddenly and who knows the ruin that both can bring?' (Prov. 24:21–2). There are some proverbs which are condemnations, often using repetition: 'The evil have no future; the lamp of the wicked will go out' (Prov. 24:20). There are some which make a contrast and are known as antithetical comparisons: 'The wicked earn no real gain, but those who sow righteousness get a true reward' (Prov. 11:18). There are commands: 'Leave the presence of a fool, for there you do not find words of knowledge' (Prov. 14:7); and there are antithetical commands: 'Lay aside immaturity, and live, and walk in the way of insight' (Prov. 9:6). There are many similes which can be spotted by the use of 'like' or 'as', for example Proverbs 26:14: 'As a door turns on its hinges, so does a lazy person in bed.' There are also metaphors, for example Proverbs 15:19 where the metaphor of thorns is used: 'The way of the lazy is overgrown with thorns, but the path of the upright is a level highway.' We also find numerical proverbs, an activity related to a liking for lists, for example Proverbs 30:18–19: 'Three things are too wonderful for me; four I do not understand: the way of an eagle in the sky, the way of a snake on a rock, the way of a ship on the high seas, and the way of a man with a girl.'

Of course, the book of Proverbs does not only contain proverbs. It also contains longer 'Instructions', often thought to parallel Instructions from Egypt (see Chapter 7). R. N. Whybray in his commentary finds ten Instructions in Proverbs 1—9 which take the form of addresses from father to son(s) about moral issues, particularly to avoid evil company and to beware of loose women (1:8–19; 2:1–22; 3:1–12; 3:21–35; 4:1–9; 4:10–19; 4:20–7; 5:1–23; 6:20–35; 7:1–27). He argues that it is unlikely that these are ten sections of one Instruction since they lack structure as a group and are rather repetitive. Rather, they are separate pieces of Instruction, representing Israelite attempts to establish an Instruction genre along Egyptian lines.

Proverbs also contains small amounts of autobiographical narrative where we read of the author's experience, for example in the description of the loose woman in Proverbs 7:6–9: 'For at the window of my house I looked out through my lattice, and I saw among the simple ones, I observed among the youths, a young man without sense, passing along the street near her corner, taking the road to her house in the twilight, in the evening, at the time of night and darkness'; and in Proverbs 24:30–4 in a cautionary tale about laziness. Another form found chiefly in Proverbs 1—9 is the hymnic description of wisdom personified as a woman and as the creative principle alongside God, as in Proverbs 1:20–33 and chapter 8. At first she is portrayed as a woman speaking to passers-by in public places, calling to them to accept the gifts she has to offer. She is clearly here a counterpart to the loose woman, described above in Proverbs 7:6–9. However, in Proverbs 8, notably in verses 22–31, she takes on a new dimension as it becomes clear that she is alongside God, the first of his creative acts and present during the creation of the world (see discussion below). Thus wisdom is linked to the order of the world, it is a fundamental part of its structure and the way it is governed: 'The Lord created me at the beginning of his work, the first of his acts of long ago. Ages ago I was set up, at the first, before the beginning of the earth' (8:22).

Content

The content of the book of Proverbs is also diverse, notably among the proverbs themselves. We find many proverbs regarding poverty and wealth (Whybray, 1990) – as today, it was a prime concern to have enough money to be comfortable, without necessarily striving for great wealth. So we find proverbs such as 10:15: 'The wealth of the rich is their fortress; the poverty of the poor is their ruin.' Many proverbs point out the dangers of falling into poverty, particularly if one is lazy: 'The lazy do not roast their game, but the diligent obtain precious wealth' (Prov. 12:27); and the proverbs do not appear to have much time for such people: 'The poor are disliked even by their neighbours, but the rich have many friends' (Prov. 14:20); although they do not lack a humanitarian concern: 'Those who oppress the poor insult their Maker, but those who are kind to the needy honour him' (Prov. 14:31). And there are higher things to be striven for than just money: 'A good name is to be chosen rather than great riches, and favour is better than silver or gold' (Prov. 22:1). There are warnings against a lottery-type mentality: 'Wealth hastily gotten will dwindle, but those who gather little by little will increase it' (Prov. 13:11). There are also proverbs on many other subjects, most of them involving a contrast – e.g. the wise person and the fool, the righteous and the wicked. There are proverbs concerning laziness and the importance of hard work and about pride and humility. There are proverbs about words and the power of speech for good or ill, warning of the dangers of gossip and foolish babbling, and, conversely, commending the power of a careful choice of words. Many involve decision-making, planning and choosing the right path. There is interest in family relationships – between husband and wife, between parents and children – and in wider circles of friends and neighbours, masters and servants, kings and rulers. All the emotions are found – hopes and fears, anger, joy and sorrow. The proverbs are full of observations on human behaviour: 'Anxiety weighs down the human heart, but a good word cheers it up' (Prov. 12:25).

The book of Proverbs is a veritable compendium of choices and advice to aid the would-be wise person to tread carefully the path of wisdom – love is better than hatred, kindness and generosity rather than selfish greed, humility is better than pride and hope better than despair. Some proverbs draw comparisons from the natural world to illuminate human behaviour: 'Better to meet a she-bear robbed of its cubs than to confront a fool immersed in folly' (Prov. 17:12); and 'A continual dripping on a rainy day and a contentious wife are alike: to restrain her is to restrain the wind or to grasp oil in the right hand' (Prov. 27:16).

Themes

This list of the various subjects covered by the proverbs does not do justice to the more profound themes that can be drawn out from the literature and which might be seen to characterise wisdom at a more basic level. A principal theme is that of order in the world. In Proverbs, we have what is essentially a positive evaluation of an order that can be found in the world through human experience. Proverbs is characterised by the quest for analogies of an essentially practical nature. The proverbs gather data about human nature that eventually form patterns that can be relied upon and so a picture of an ordered world starts to emerge. The build-up of a fund of observations that represented truth and were available to all meant that the wise person could attempt to live according to this order in behaviour and relationships with others.

However, there was seen to be an ambiguity in events – and this is a second theme. Sometimes experience was contradictory – and the proverbs make allowance for this. An example is where a proverb sees silence as a virtue and too much talk as a negative thing, but then goes on to suggest that when people are silent they could just as well be wise as a fool – one cannot tell until they speak (Prov. 17:27–8). On a more profound religious level, there was seen to be a limit to the quest for order and certainty. Beyond that limit was the realm of Yahweh, which was less knowable than the human sphere. So, we find proverbs such as 16:1: 'The plans of the mind belong to mortals, but the answer of the tongue is from the Lord.' A tension thus starts to appear, even in the oldest sections of the book of Proverbs, between human knowledge and the ultimate meaning of events which is unknowable apart from Yahweh.

A third theme is that of punishment and reward – to the

wicked, the fool, the sluggard or the evildoer punishment will come, but to the wise, the upright, the hard worker and the diligent rewards will be great. There is a just and individual accounting system in operation. It is a simple choice to be made by the one who wishes to learn – either that such people can take the path of wisdom that is smooth and straight and leads to all good things or they can take the path to folly which is full of pitfalls and covered with thorns. There are material rewards associated with these two paths: wealth is the result of wisdom, poverty comes to the unsuspecting fool. Thus, 'The crooked of mind do not prosper, and the perverse of tongue fall into calamity' (Prov. 17:20). While there is a recognition that the wicked do sometimes prosper, this is seen as a fleeting thing, for example, Proverbs 11:18: 'The wicked earn no real gain, but those who sow righteousness get a true reward.' The rewards are not only monetary ones; they include happiness, fulfilment and longevity.

This leads us to the fourth theme of life as the supreme good. Life means, in the language of Proverbs, a prosperous, materially rewarded and long existence characterised by good health, good deeds, many friends, children, possessions and a commitment to wisdom: 'Happy are those who find wisdom, and those who get understanding ... Long life is in her right hand; in her left hand are riches and honour' (Prov. 3:13, 16). There is no lengthy preoccupation with death in the book of Proverbs (unlike Job and Ecclesiastes); rather, a happy and successful life is at the forefront of concern.

There is a fifth theme of what might be termed confidence in wisdom: the search for knowledge is the chief goal of life which all can acquire and should acquire to be on the path of life rather than on the path of death. Wisdom is on offer to all, not to an exclusive group, and this is because it links up with a profound order to be found in the world. There is a real confidence in the doctrine of retribution, that rewards come to those who deserve them and disaster to the wicked, which was not shared by the authors of the more questioning wisdom books. Good and bad actions also have a broader application than just to individual lives – they affect the entire social order, e.g. Proverbs 11:11: 'By the blessing of the upright a city is exalted, but it is overthrown by the mouth of the wicked.'

The final theme is the personification of wisdom. It is clear from Proverbs 1—9 that at the heart of the wisdom exercise is personified Wisdom herself. The most important text in this connection is Proverbs 8:22f. Here we find a poetic personification of the female aspect of God. Some scholars such as C. Kayatz (1966) and B. Lang (1975) have sought a separate goddess figure behind this personification positing that this figure was originally a female consort of God, such as was found in neighbouring religions. Kayatz, for example, finds the origin of the genre of 'wisdom speech' as found here and in Proverbs 1:20-33 in the Egyptian self-praising speech by a god or goddess, while Lang argues for pre-exilic Israelite goddess imagery that has been demythologised. An interesting parallel to the figure of Wisdom in Proverbs is found in the Egyptian concept of Ma'at, an abstract principle of order, truth and justice that was accorded divine status as a goddess (see Kayatz who points to a particular parallel between Proverbs 3:16, the description of wisdom as holding long life in her right hand and riches and honour in her left, and pictorial representations of Ma'at which represent her as holding in her hands symbols of life, riches and honour). However, Ma'at does not make a direct appeal to humanity as Wisdom does. Majority scholarly opinion does not see the Israelite figure of Wisdom as a separate goddess, preferring to interpret the imagery within a monotheistic framework as a poetic personification. Even if some mythological influences are allowed, the portrayal is, rather, seen as a literary device to describe the female aspect of God (von Rad, [1970] 1972; Camp, 1985). A few scholars (e.g. Ringgren, 1947) see Wisdom as a hypostasis (i.e., a separate entity from God of the nature of an angelic being). However, the majority see her as a poetic personification of attributes of God. It is often thought that while the figure of Wisdom does become a hypostasis in later texts such as the Wisdom of Solomon (see Chapter 9), this is not the case in Proverbs.

It is clear from Proverbs 8 that Wisdom is Yahweh's creature and therefore created by God, one whose existence is wholly derived from God, but at the same time distinguishable from the godhead. She is described as being in existence before all God's works of creation and is the first-born of all creatures (Prov. 8:22). She is not herself the creator, but is present during the creative process. The relationship between her and the creator is described as one of joyful interaction: 'Then I was beside him, like a master worker; and I was daily his delight, rejoicing before him always' (8:30). In the whole passage an interesting pattern is found. In Proverbs 8:22–31 the creation of Wisdom is described. This includes her relationship with God – 'rejoicing before him always, rejoicing in his inhabited world' (8:30–1a) – but also her relationship with humans, 'delighting in the human race' (8:31). Immediately after this in verse 32 we have the specific call to humans, 'And now, my children, listen to me: happy are those who keep my ways. Hear instruction and be wise, and do not neglect it', and in verse 35, 'For whoever finds me finds life and obtains favour from the Lord; but those who miss me injure themselves; all who hate me love death.' The pattern of this poem shows a move from God to human beings, and the human need to respond to God for the acquisition of life, which is contrasted with the folly of not doing so. This poem starts on the level of the cosmo-logical God and finishes on the level of humanity. The purpose of God is to reveal himself to human beings. The purpose of wisdom is to teach and instruct humanity to find life. There is a complete interdependence of the divine and the human here. Wisdom is the process of revelation to humankind. Cosmological statements are the introduction to that wisdom which calls to humans with their will to acquire knowledge. Here we find a theological profundity in the wisdom literature that takes us to the heart of what wisdom in relationship means. We shall go on to consider other poems about the female personification of wisdom in the later wisdom books of Ben Sira and the Wisdom of Solomon where a similar pattern may be found and where the theological ideas develop further (see Chapters 8 and 9).

Context

So what kind of context(s) might the diverse material of Proverbs have had? It will be clear by now that the book of Proverbs divides into distinct sections, one clear section being Proverbs 1—9 with its number of Instructions and more theological reflection; another being Proverbs 10:1—22:16 which consists of a succession of proverbs in no obvious order. Smaller collections follow in Proverbs 22:16—24:22; Proverbs 25—9 and 30 and 31. We need therefore to be open to the possibility of different contexts for the different sections of the book. The question is raised, however, who wrote these collections, when and for whom? Should we think in categories of authors writing specifically for an audience? While the book must have been gathered together in written form at some stage, much of the material seems likely to have had an oral origin. Much of it may be the distillation of long experience, perhaps a core of knowledge that built up over many centuries within families and wider groups. Thus while the collections as we have them now are written, these written stages need to be distinguished from earlier stages through which the material may have passed. Thus the proverbs of 10:1—22:16 have the character of folk wisdom, of the experience of many generations distilled into short, pithy sayings. They may be quite old in origin, reflecting an oral tradition that circulated within families and tribes. They may however have been written down by a more educated group, by intellectuals who could read and write and had the leisure for reflection and literary activity. Hence the theory arose of a group of sages to whom the writing down of the proverbs could be attributed, a group that might have clustered around the king and his court. However, other parts may have been literary productions from the start, especially composed for use in teaching contexts perhaps.

One of the complicating factors is that a number of different backgrounds are reflected even within one of the collections. In Proverbs 10:1—22:16, therefore, many proverbs appear to address those for whom poverty is a real danger and for whom hard work to maintain a good standard of living is essential. On the other hand, some proverbs concern the king, which has led some to believe that a court background is revealed here: for example, 'Inspired decisions are on the lips of a king; his mouth does not sin in judgment' (Prov. 16:10). Deciding between different contexts is therefore a complex issue and it would seem to be best to be open to a range of possibilities. There is also a question: how overtly theological is the context? Is proverbial wisdom primarily secular-type advice for all which then develops later on into a specifically theological context or is it imbued with a theological outlook from the start?

So we find ourselves faced with three key questions: What

kind of social context did the Proverbs have, if we bear in mind different stages through which the material passed and the different collections in the book? How are we to distinguish between oral and literary stages and their relative importance? And how is the book to be characterised theologically? At this stage it is important to note that scholarly views on this issue have changed considerably in the last decade, and so it is important to chart this change.

Social context

Let us start with the idea that much of the proverbial material has the character of traditional sayings or folk wisdom. Simple proverbs such as 'Better is a dinner of vegetables where love is than a fatted ox and hatred with it' (Prov. 15:17) are the kinds of observation that require no complex social context to explain them. Similarly, many proverbs have the nature of family wisdom, such as Proverbs 10:1, the opening proverb of the oldest collection: 'A wise child makes a glad father, but a foolish child is a mother's grief.' The numerous references to 'father' and 'mother' in the proverbial literature are best taken at face value rather than being seen, as some scholars have argued, as representing teacher and pupil in a school context. Education seems to have taken place to a certain extent within the family context. This is supported by the final chapter of Proverbs, chapter 31, which is an oracle taught to King Lemuel by his mother. Some have argued that this also provides evidence of a court context for other proverbs, especially those that mention the king (e.g. Prov. 14:28, 35; 16:12–15; 20:8, 26; 21:1), but the king-sayings do not necessarily require such a context – any person can speak of the king (Dell, 1998).

The importance of the earliest stage of the proverbial material has been stressed afresh by C. Westermann in his book *The Roots of Wisdom* ([1990] 1995). It has also been supported by parallels from other tribal societies – F. W. Golka (1993) has used African parallels to stress the early nature of wisdom as an oral folk tradition, and the subject matter of many proverbs would seem to support this. R. N. Whybray (1990) notes that many proverbs concern the need for hard work, and the danger of falling into poverty through laziness, sentiments that would hardly be fitting in circles of the rich. However, other proverbs indicate a city background – Proverbs 1—9, for example, which has the female figure of wisdom standing at the gate of the city, calling to young men in the streets. Again, different sections of the book of Proverbs indicate different contexts. There is an everyday quality to many proverbs which might be assigned to a 'family' or 'tribal' stage. Yet, it must be remembered too that this 'family' stage of proverbs is not only the earliest stage in that their use would have continued in families throughout the generations. C. V. Camp (1985) has argued, for example, that the family context would have provided a point of stability throughout the changing political fortunes of Israel into post-exilic times. R. E. Clements (1992) has recently argued that a new emphasis on morals at the Exile, when other areas of Israel's life were falling apart, led to a fresh appraisal of the wisdom literature on an individual and family level.

However, whilst much of the proverbial material no doubt originated in the family, most people would not be sufficiently literate to preserve these sayings in a written context such as we have in Proverbs. Traditional wisdom must by some process have been collected and written down. We know that in Egypt wisdom sayings were used for education in schools. Could this have been the case in Israel? Here we enter a heated debate which ranges from scholars who deny the existence of schools in ancient Israel (Crenshaw, 1998) to those who consider that they existed in every town and city (Lemaire, 1981). For many scholars there may have been a kind of court school in Jerusalem for the education of the élite, but outside this it is felt to be unlikely (Crenshaw). However, we have to remember that there were shrines and cultic centres outside Jerusalem and that we have evidence of educated priestly families living in towns outside Jerusalem (e.g. Jeremiah at Anathoth). Amos and Micah too were both from outside Jerusalem and scholars find in them more literary artistry than their country background would seem to require. This raises the possibility that there might have been simply a few educated men in a town (some of whom would conceivably have been connected to the temple, possibly as priests) who gave instruction to those who had the potential to be leaders of society themselves. This kind of model would complement that of a school in Jerusalem, bound to court or temple, where material would be cherished and collected and written down. Whether there was a distinct group called 'sages' is another question – it is quite likely that tasks were carefully delineated and that sages had the task of recording and collecting material; whether they were also government administrators in the same way that they were in Egypt is another question.

In this area we find some real shift in scholarly opinion in the last decade. The view, based largely on the Egyptian context, that wisdom was most likely promulgated through court schools designed to educate future leaders and administrators has largely fallen from favour. It was argued that at the time of Solomon there was a kind of enlightenment, an expansion of court and state and the need for administrators to run that state, the building of the temple, prosperity through trade and also a flowering of culture and writing (Heaton, 1974). Heaton argued for the wisdom literature as the product of a heightened confidence in human achievement that accompanied the Solomonic Enlightenment. He posited the growth of an administrative class, largely separate from the rest of society, which accounted for the lack of interest in covenant and law in the wisdom literature and its rather secular character. Only later, when the money to support the administration ran out, did the wisdom enterprise change and become more overtly theological. The proverbs that refer to the king were seen to provide evidence of a court context for some proverbial material (Humphreys, 1978) but more significantly parallels between Proverbs 22:17—24:22 and the Egyptian Instruction of Amenemope, published in 1923, led scholars to suppose that this section of Proverbs and, probably more, was used as a school textbook for the training of young men at court. The Egyptian instructions contain practical advice for successful living, and they are largely written by or for Pharaohs or their senior administrators. Schools in Egypt were specifically designed to train young men for administrative roles in the state and instructions were used as part of that educational process.

There is no doubt that an educated, literate group must have been responsible for the writing down of proverbs and that the time of Solomon may have been one in which such activity took place, since Solomon is traditionally regarded as the patron of wisdom and epitome of the wise man. However, as I have mentioned, the description of Solomon in 1 Kings 10 would suggest that he was engaged in a fairly primitive kind of wisdom somewhat unlike what we have in the book of Proverbs. This has led to the suggestion that maybe the court of Hezekiah (Prov. 25:1) rather later on in Israel's history would have provided a more suitable context for the collection and preservation of material. While this suggestion may have some credibility, the court context in general is thought by some recent scholars to have been overstressed. Questions are raised in particular about the strength of the Egyptian parallels. Although cultural influence between the two nations is likely this does not mean that the institutions were identical. Israel was a much smaller country than Egypt and probably could not support and did not need an administrative machine of the size of the Egyptian one. Furthermore, although most scholars are convinced by the parallels between Proverbs 22:17—24:22 and the Egyptian Instruction of Amenemope, a few think that this has been overstated (Whybray, 1994b). Whybray argues that this section does not consist of thirty proverbs (thus contesting the reading of 'thirty' in the statement in Proverbs 22:20: 'Have I not written for you thirty sayings of admonition and knowledge') that match the thirty-line Instruction of Amenemope, but rather that separate units of instruction are to be found here that may contain reminiscences of, but are not directly dependent upon, the Egyptian prototype (see discussion in Chapter 7). If we bear in mind the possibility of separate contexts for different sections of Proverbs, even if such extra-biblical parallels are convincing for this particular section of Proverbs, they may not anyway hold the key to understanding the contexts reflected by other parts of the book. Thus while there may well have been a 'school tradition', as Heaton terms it, an interest in literature spanning the centuries, the work of the educated, this may not mean that it was necessarily the preserve of a courtly group. Rather, the varied backgrounds reflected by the proverbs suggest that this collection is much more than a manual for would-be administrators or a school textbook. It may well have come together over a period of time, and material would have been used afresh in changing contexts.

Literary-critical concerns

The nature of the proverbial material is another factor in the shifting views of scholars on contextual matters. It was supposed that much of the material was literary from the start and the oral stage was not perceived to be as significant as it was once thought to be by older scholars, and as it is now thought to be by more recent ones. A complex view was that there was a development from simple to more complicated forms of proverbs – from one-limbed sayings to multi-limbed ones and from proverbial forms to instruction forms (McKane, 1970). So literary forms were developed well beyond the simple proverb to become a complex literary exercise, and the book of Proverbs was thought to provide evidence of that development. Narrative texts were included in this development – the Joseph narrative, with Joseph as the exemplar of the wise counsellor at Pharaoh's court, and the Succession Narrative, telling of the succession to the throne, for example, were seen as products of the Solomonic enlightenment, the work of courtiers who were close to the events described. It was also held that the 'J' (Jahwistic) source of the Pentateuch may have found its context here as a celebration of the nation's history, reflecting the confidence of the national pride generated by this age of prosperity, written to preserve tribal stories that were in danger of being lost. However, many would take issue with this supposition nowadays. For example, R. N. Whybray's book, *The Composition of the Book of Proverbs* (1994a), has found much uncertainty in the attempt to locate and date literary developments such as those from one-limbed to multi-limbed sayings and prefers to see different genres such as 'instruction' and 'maxims' as different strands of the tradition.

A related problem is that we do not know precisely when the transition from oral to literary transmission took place, nor do we know that it was in fact a strict line of development from one to the other. Archaeological discoveries of inscriptions suggest that writing became more widespread in the eighth century BC and we have the evidence in Proverbs 25:1 that the officials of Hezekiah copied that particular collection from Proverbs 25—9 at least. We have evidence of literary activity at the time of Josiah with the finding of the law book in the temple (2 Kings 22:8–10). We have evidence too of the use of proverbs in other non-wisdom books, although we do not know whether we are to treat such wisdom usage as primary influence or as later redaction. We can never be sure whether a wisdom motif was part of a prophet's own vocabulary or whether in fact it was a literary addendum by those shaping the book in more literary circles. It may be, therefore, that the more literary production of wisdom books such as the collections we find in Proverbs is a rather later phenomenon than Solomon's era, but itself a gradual process. This is by no means however to deny the antiquity of wisdom which may well have been circulating in families, in communities, at court and in Israelite life in general from an early period. There may have been older influence from wisdom on narrative writing or in prophetic oracles (see Chapter 6) – highly likely if it was a language of ordinary people, a way of understanding the world and attempting to control the chaos of reality. But also, as wisdom flowered as a literary activity in more intellectual circles, it may well have become associated with more overtly religious or priestly circles, thus leading to its development in more theological directions as reflected in Proverbs 1—9.

Theological character

This leads us on to our question about how we should characterise the wisdom literature – was it once a secular and later on a theological activity? Again, this view of wisdom's development was held by scholars of a decade or so ago and linked with the idea of court origins. The natural corollary of the view that saw wisdom as a training for life in a secular context was to stress those aspects of the material that were less theological. G. von Rad ([1958–61] 1962a) posited the idea that a simple quest from the human side to find patterns in life, order in the world and to illuminate human behaviour became gradually more God-centred. McKane (1970) put forward the idea of a gradually more theologically advanced content and context. Proverbs 1—9 was seen to be the most theological section of Proverbs and was regarded therefore as the very latest part of the book. In it wisdom takes on more profound dimensions in that God is described as having founded the world by wisdom and wisdom is personified as a woman who calls to young men to follow her path (Prov. 8) rather than the path of folly (Prov. 7). The female personification of wisdom is God's wisdom, created at the beginning, the mediator of creation. However, even within this section, Instructions, as paralleled in Egypt, were seen as primarily serving an educational function with a religious element being added later (Whybray, 1965).

Clearly, the word 'secular' is inappropriate to characterise Israelite thought, given the religious world-view of the Israelites in general. However, the idea that the proverbs were essentially common sense as opposed to having their starting point in religious ideas about God is the point being made here. It is true that there is no revelation in history as we find elsewhere in the Old Testament. And yet it is not true to say that God is not present. He is there at the limits of the quest for knowledge and he is also the imparter of knowledge of the created world in particular through the figure of wisdom in Proverbs 8. It is often overlooked that in Proverbs 10:1—22:16 those proverbs which mention God are mixed amongst other proverbs in which there is no mention, as in Proverbs 16:1, 'The plans of the mind belong to mortals, but the answer of the tongue is from the Lord', and Proverbs 19:21, 'The human mind may devise many plans, but it is the purpose of the Lord that will be established.' The more theological viewpoint of wisdom, as shown in Proverbs 1—9, is often thought to have developed out of somewhat of a crisis and a loss of confidence in human ability. This is not the only viewpoint however. Some scholars such as H. H. Schmid (1966) saw wisdom as having been quite religious from the start – like Egyptian and Mesopotamian wisdom, he argued, there was a divine order that matched the human order that could be found through the wisdom quest. He argued that although this gradually became a more explicit theology as reflected in Proverbs 1—9, there are religious verses in 'old wisdom' that betray this religious character, another example being Proverbs 14:26–7: 'In the fear of the Lord one has strong confidence, and one's children will have a refuge. The fear of the Lord is a fountain of life, so that one may avoid the snares of death.' Schmid argued that there was a development from a more theological wisdom into a more human-centred wisdom, as expressed in rather moralistic terms about right and wrong which led to a later association of wisdom with law. This viewpoint sees the entire development of wisdom the other way around from von Rad and McKane.

It may be that rather than arguing for a development from one to another, it is probably better, in the same way as we saw different contexts being appropriate for different sections of Proverbs and at different times, to argue that there was an ongoing tension between the human-sided wisdom and the God-given dimension. This tension, although possibly more obvious in late material, characterises wisdom from earliest times and is, in my view, the key that unlocks an understanding of the nature of the wisdom quest. We find both to varying degrees in the book of Proverbs and in wisdom in general. The two are bound up together in that human experience is not divorced from the realm of God who stands behind it as the orderer and creator, nor is God divorced from humanity in that he reveals himself in all human experience and in the created world. Thus wisdom's theology of creation is revealed (Perdue, 1994) – the order found in human society, relationships and nature reflects the order of the world as created by God. As mentioned above, there are possible parallels with the Egyptian Ma'at, the principle of order, justice and truth. God stands at the heart of this order and ultimately has the answers which will be mediated through Wisdom to those who wish to follow her path. The figure of Wisdom in Proverbs 8, as we saw above, stands at the meeting point of the heavenly and the earthly and forms a link between the created order and the practical quest for wisdom. We might ask about the context of this more theological emphasis – it may latterly have belonged in groups undertaking religious training, for example in temple schools (Doll, 1985), although its context is probably more diverse than that, given its earlier roots.

As for the relative development of the different strands, it looks as though the theological developments were taken further in the post-exilic period, but that does not preclude there being a religious aspect to proverbs from the start. Even in Proverbs 1—9, as we have seen, there could be older mythological allusions lying behind the figure of wisdom. R. N. Whybray (1994a) has pointed to the fact that we need to be open to the idea of parallel and even contradictory developments. Society is never represented by one

view at one time, rather there may have been pockets of more theological reflection existing alongside more practical concerns. We
have perhaps been too tied to developmental models in general and
need to rethink such ideas (Dell, 1997).

3: JOB

Who has the wisdom to number the clouds? Or who can tilt the waterskins of the heavens? (Job 38:37)

The book of Job is generally dated later than Proverbs – any time from the Exile in the sixth century to the fourth century BC. However, as we have seen, Proverbs is itself multi-layered and some of the final redaction of Proverbs may have occurred towards the exilic period or later. The book of Job is very unlike Proverbs on a formal level in that it contains few maxims and it has its own dialogue genre. Furthermore, the book is a more literary composition in its entirety than Proverbs. Their thought-worlds may well have coincided and Job may well represent a re-action away from that of Proverbs rather than a distinct development beyond its ideas. While Proverbs maintained an optimistic belief in the doctrine of retribution, Job is seen to be a refutation of this. Job represents the experience of the righteous man to whom suffering unexpectedly came. He had done all in his power to lead life according to the principles of wisdom and certainly did not deserve what came to him. Did this not show that the exhortations to lead a good life in order to expect material rewards found in Proverbs were bankrupt? Similarly, although there is the same view of God as creator that we find in Proverbs, does the God of Job not simply reveal that the creator spends most of his time doing great things that no one can understand (Job 38—41) and that whilst fearing God is probably wise it does not lead to real understanding?

In this chapter we shall ask what the main literary, historical and theological features of the book of Job are. Should we include it as wisdom literature according to the criteria of form, content and context that we have set up? Furthermore, how did the book come together as a literary whole? First, however, I will give an outline of the story.

Outline

Job consists of a prose narrative which surrounds a poetic dialogue. The prose story tells a simple tale of a man who 'feared God and turned away from evil' (Job 1:1). Despite his goodness, calamity strikes. The story tells of a wager that took place in heaven between God and Satan, a scenario about which Job knows nothing. This wager was explicitly designed to test Job. Would he waver from his faith in God if all his possessions and loved ones were taken away from him? Would he then waver if he was struck down by a festering disease? The story is then about disinterested righteousness – 'Does Job fear God for nothing?' asks Satan (Job 1:9), and so God lets him test Job's patience. And he seemingly passes the test. When his wife advises him to 'Curse God and die' (Job 2:9) he does no such thing. He says humbly, 'Shall we receive the good at the hand of God, and not receive the bad?' (Job 2:10) He accepts all that comes to him, good and bad alike. And so at the end of the book in the prose epilogue he is rewarded with a new set of children and twice as many material possessions as he had before.

But I have left out from this account the dialogue section which is surrounded by the prose story. This section begins in chapter 3 and has Job bursting in with a complaint that sounds remarkably like a curse: 'After that Job opened his mouth and cursed the day of his birth. And Job said, "Let the day perish in which I was born and the night that said, 'A man-child is conceived.' Let that day be darkness. May God above not seek it, or light shine upon it. Let gloom and deep darkness claim it. Let clouds settle upon it; let the blackness of the day terrify it." ' (Job 3:3–5) This is a frightening description which comes from the depths of a person's despair. Suddenly the character of Job comes alive. No longer do we have a pious, bland character who simply accepts good and bad; here we have someone protesting at none other than God himself. Any thought of Satan is gone – it is God who in Job's eyes has inflicted this undeserved suffering and he is to be held to account. Job wrestles to understand and at this point his three friends try to comfort him with conventional answers to his questions. But Job's world has been turned upside down – no longer are these answers sufficient. So a debate that centres on the doctrine of retribution begins – the friends say

Job must have sinned and so he is being punished, a stock answer that had certainly been around since the Exile. Job however maintains his innocence throughout – he did not deserve this suffering, of that he is sure. The speeches of the friends get gradually shorter and those of Job get longer as he gains ground and as he leaves their arguments behind. It becomes a confrontation between Job and God, and eventually Job's only plea is for God to appear to him to justify his ways.

At this point a fourth 'friend' appears named Elihu – one who has had no introduction, and gives his opinion, largely repeating the line of the other friends, but also anticipating the next scene in which God eventually appears. This has the effect of spoiling the climax to a certain extent. However, at last God appears, but only to ignore Job's questions and ask him where he was at creation and why he thinks he has all the answers. One could argue that at least Job gets some kind of answer, even though it is not the one he was expecting. H. H. Rowley (1970) argues that it is the presence of God that silences Job and causes him to repent, and he likens Job to Psalm 73 where the psalmist is distressed at the prosperity of the wicked but then goes into the sanctuary and perceives their end. Others such as C. G. Jung ([1952] 1954) argue that the kind of God found in Job is incredible, unbelievable and in the end tyrannical – he asks what kind of God we are being expected to believe in here. Is it a God who plays with human beings as if for sport and teases them with unanswered questions?

Clearly then, much of Job is about humankind's relationship to God and vice versa. A theological profundity has entered the debate here which involves the whole question of suffering and its meaning and the nature of the Godhead. There is also the matter of protest. Job wages a protest against God's treatment of him and it seems that he is silenced, except for the existence of one verse in Job 42:7 which states that God is angry with the friends because 'you have not spoken of me what is right, as my servant Job has'. Here it seems that Job's protest is being confirmed – Job was perhaps right to question. He grew in his faith through his suffering; he no longer accepts pat answers such as the friends tried to give him. Job then intercedes on their behalf. However, here we have returned to the

prose tale, so perhaps originally these words referred back to the prologue where Job uttered his pious words about receiving good and
evil alike from God.

What I have just presented is a holistic-type reading of Job,
trying to make sense of what seem to be disjointed parts of the book
in the effort to read it as a consistent whole. This is an approach of
interest in modern scholarship and represented in commentaries
such as that by N. C. Habel (1985). It has sprung from uncertainty
regarding the process by which the text came together and from
increased interest in the final form of biblical books and it has yielded
some interesting conclusions regarding overall structure and plot
development (Hoffman, 1981; Habel, 1985). Habel, for example, has
found a striking coherence in the overall pattern of Job, including
sections such as the Elihu speeches as an integral part of the plot,
functioning as a foil to the speeches of God. Some scholars are
sceptical of deciding earlier and later versions of the book in the
manner of older scholars such as N. Snaith (1968). For example,
D. J. A. Clines (1989) describes such literary-critical problems as
insoluble and prefers not to speculate on them. However, other
scholars, myself included, think that in order fully to understand the
different levels on which the book can be read, an account needs to
be taken of the literary history of the book.

Literary-critical analysis

This brings us to a literary-critical analysis of the book of
Job. It is generally agreed that the book is disjointed and widely held
that an older folk tale was later filled with the dialogue section – the
speeches of Job and the friends and the speeches of God – to make
up the bulk of the book. It was then subjected to a second stage of
additions consisting of the Elihu speeches, chapter 28 and possibly
the second speech of God. How do scholars work this out? Well, the
prologue and epilogue are in prose and the dialogue sections in
poetry – this makes a natural break. Most scholars have thought that
the prose sections are earlier, but a few have thought that they were
later additions to an existing dialogue, put around the dialogue to
provide a context for otherwise abstract musings on the relationship
between God and human beings. Others have thought that the two

existed independently and that they were brought together at a later stage of the development of the canon of scripture. However, we do have evidence in Ezekiel 14:14, 20 that a figure called Job was known to be a righteous man along with Noah and Daniel. In the prose story this aspect of Job's character – his righteousness and constancy in the face of disaster – is emphasised, whereas in the dialogue these are not at the forefront in any way. This would suggest to me that the prose sections are earlier. There are no decisive linguistic reasons for dating one earlier than the other, except that the prose section is considerably simpler Hebrew, and on the supposition that simple precedes more complicated, it is likely to be earlier. The dialogue section is generally dated around the fourth century BC and contains many Aramaisms which are thought to have influenced the Hebrew language at this time and after. Also the dialogue section without the prose section does not make a great deal of sense – one would expect the context to be given first. However, there are problems with the prose framework too in that in many ways it does not match the dialogue. For example, it shows Job as patient in the face of suffering while in the dialogue he is the opposite; and it shows Job as the victim of a bet between God and Satan (although neither in the dialogue nor in the epilogue is Satan to be seen). Further, it introduces three friends who sit with Job in comforting silence, who then increase to four later in the dialogue and are anything but silent, verbosity being a key element of their speeches. Finally, after the theory of just retribution has been decisively overturned in the dialogue, the epilogue then has Job rewarded with twice as many cattle and goods that he had before, just as the theory would dictate. What are we to make of this? Did whoever added the dialogue not have a full understanding of what was going on? This seems highly unlikely in the light of the fact that Job is widely regarded as a pinnacle of Hebrew writing. It is more likely, in my view, that this was deliberate – the author of the dialogue was providing a foil for the prologue and epilogue, saying in effect that people do not generally react to suffering in the way that the prologue suggests; that friends can often be less than helpful and offering up the happy ending as a kind of ironic postscript to the discussion that has been under way.

Historical concerns

There is a folk tale feel to the story of Job in the stylised numbers of his possessions and in the parallelism between the prologue and the epilogue. Does this mean he is not a historical figure? Again, scholars are divided on this question. Job may well be a paradigm, used to illustrate a moral dilemma or he may have had a very remote historical existence. The Ezekiel reference helps to reinforce the arguments for his historicity, given that the other figures mentioned are presented as historical. Jewish interpreters counted Job among the patriarchs and for a long time the whole book was thought to come from that period, although not so by scholars today. There is no historical certainty over the location of Uz – it is probably the area of Edom, just south of Judah – and it does seem odd that the story is set outside the bounds of Israel. If Job was an Israelite patriarch, this does not quite tie together. If, however, he is a paradigm from a more international wisdom tradition, this might make more sense.

On the question of dating the book, scholars have suggested everything from the twelfth to the second century BC. Nowadays scholars tend to opt for between the sixth century and the second (although, see Wolfers (1995) for a seventh-century date). It seems likely to me that there may have been a tale going around certainly by the sixth century – witness Ezekiel (who was at work during the Exile, 587 BC onwards) – about a righteous man (Ezekiel 14:14, 20). Then at the Exile the whole issue of just retribution for sin came up and so the dialogue seeks to address that question, not in a corporate way, but in reference to the individual, with which much of the wisdom tradition is concerned. It seems likely that the dialogue section was composed between the fifth and the fourth centuries but not later, since it does not show traces of Greek influence from the third century and after. However, the timeless quality of the book makes dating a difficult task. It seems most naturally to belong after the Exile, as it attacks the view that suffering must be a direct result of sin and must represent punishment from God, the key theme of exilic theology, but we cannot be more precise than that.

Theological overview

The traditional view is that the prologue and epilogue chiefly treat the issue of disinterested righteousness – will Job remain steadfast whatever happens to him? This is of course based on the wager between God and Satan and affects the whole way in which we read the book. We see Job as the victim of a trial in that God is not really like that but he is doing it just to test Job. It seeks to exonerate God and yet it raises doubts about his integrity. Without this heavenly debate, the prologue serves to show the attitude of a patient man in the face of calamity from God. He is squarely to blame through natural disaster and this is the point from which the debate departs. Various other theological themes are raised in the rest of the book. The dialogue concerns chiefly the doctrine of just deserts, the friends maintaining that Job must have sinned and therefore he is being punished; Job maintaining that he is innocent and that he has not deserved his miserable fate. The speeches of Job climax in his demanding an answer from God and using legal language to try to force him into the dock. This raises the more profound theological issue of the relationship between God and human beings and questions whether humans can have a meaningful relationship with God given that such arbitrary things as Job's suffering seem to happen. This question is raised but not really answered in the speeches of God, where God the creator puts Job in his place and asks where he was at creation to think that he has all the answers. However, Job seems to be exonerated in 42:7 where the friends are told off by God for not having spoken right of God as Job has. This suggests that it is better to have a good argument with God than simply to accept the status quo and fall into dry repetition of ideas. Finally, we have the 'happily ever after' epilogue which asserts that the righteous are rewarded after all. There is even a new set of children for Job to replace his former offspring – what more could anyone want? Or is there just a hint of irony in that?

Job as a wisdom book

The book of Job is traditionally seen as a wisdom book, but one of a very different kind from Proverbs. It is 'wisdom in revolt', coming from a time after the Exile when belief in traditional categories, such as the doctrine of retribution which we saw to be so central to Proverbs, had become sterile. So Job is thought to belong to development from within wisdom itself which questions the simple answers of the earlier wisdom exercise. However, before simply accepting this, we need to go back to our criteria for defining wisdom. Clearly, if we choose a broad definition of wisdom, such as 'an approach to reality', Job fits the category, but then, as we saw, so does much else. But if we use our criteria of form, content and context of a similar nature and amount as in the book of Proverbs to determine whether the book should be included as wisdom literature we have a stronger starting point.

Form

When we look at forms in Job we find some proverbs although they occur rarely, e.g. Job 17:5: 'Those who denounce friends for reward – the eyes of their children will fail.' Proverbs are more often formulated as rhetorical questions, e.g. Job 6:5–6: 'Does the wild ass bray over its grass, or the ox low over its fodder?' (cf. Job 8:11–12; 12:12). We find a few isolated numerical sayings (Job 5:19–21; 13:20–2; 33:4–30) and didactic poems, in the speeches of Job's friends for example, and in the hymn to wisdom in chapter 28 – all good wisdom genres. However, a number of forms are missing from Job – for example, there is no autobiographical narrative where the author suddenly appears with an 'I'. Even more significantly, however, the main forms of Job do not feature in Proverbs, such as the dialogue form in which the main body of the book is cast, and the prose narrative, the debate and lament; nor does Proverbs contain any material directly addressed to God or directly spoken by God as Job does. Small wisdom forms are therefore to be found in Job, but we have to ask ourselves if these are enough on their own to characterise the whole book as wisdom literature. When we start to look through the book we find that many forms from other areas of Israelite life feature, particularly lament forms from the Psalms and a number of legal genres. Does this not suggest that Job is rather an eclectic work and on a strict definition of wisdom literature fails to meet up to the criteria?

Content

There is little question that the book of Job airs a traditional wisdom concern, the doctrine of retribution. However, it is immediately apparent that Job questions in contrast to the serene authoritativeness of earlier wisdom. His ideas break outside the bounds of traditional wisdom beliefs, even though they may have their starting point there. Furthermore, the teaching of the doctrine of retribution is not solely a wisdom concern – at the time of the Exile it was a key issue for prophets such as Jeremiah and Ezekiel when trying to understand the nation's fate. We identified six key themes in Proverbs that seemed to characterise the content of wisdom and we need to explore how Job matches up to those. The first was order in the world, whether or not it could be found and whether it is to be gained by human experience or from God alone. In contrast to the confidence found in Proverbs, Job represents a shattering of faith in such an order, a critique of the traditional wisdom stance, e.g. Job 9:2–7: 'Indeed I know that this is so; but how can a mortal be just before God? If one wished to contend with him, one could not answer him once in a thousand' (vv. 2–3). The same is true on the second issue of the ambiguity of events and of the meaning of life. Rather than an acceptance of a certain ambiguity in Proverbs, which nevertheless does not threaten the relationship between humans and the divine, ambiguity moves centre-stage in Job to become negative and to throw into question the very foundations on which Job's relationship with God is based. He strains to obtain a deeper understanding (e.g. Job 10:2–17: 'I will say to God, Do not condemn me; let me know why you contend against me' (v. 2)), and yet his questions are not directly answered.

In Proverbs we found a third theme of punishment and reward which was seen to work in a fair way. Of course, in Job it is the fact that doctrine of retribution seems to be broken, in that punishments and rewards are going to the wrong people, that leads to the suffering in the first place and the questioning in the second. God's actions towards good and bad people alike seem to be essentially arbitrary (Job 12:13–25). The first section of this passage seems to praise God for his 'wisdom and strength', 'counsel and understanding', and yet it becomes clear that he is responsible for all kinds of actions, some of which make sense and some of which do not: 'He leads priests away stripped, and overthrows the mighty. He deprives of speech those who are trusted, and takes away the discernment of the elders' (vv. 19–20). The fourth theme was life as the supreme good. In Job there is never the idea of suicide, but he curses the day of his birth, wishes he had never been born and wishes he was dead – all in one chapter (Job 3). This is because his life has been made a mockery. Therefore there is some question as to how 'good' he thinks life is: 'Why is light given to one who cannot see the way, whom God has fenced in? For my sighing comes like my bread, and my groanings are poured out like water' (Job 3:23–4). His previous faith in the doctrine of retribution has been shattered, and with that his trust in God: he believed God to be predictable and now he sees that he is not. This has led to a tension between his old beliefs to which he naturally clings and his present experience which contradicts all that he formerly knew. The fifth theme was confidence in wisdom, i.e. in the quest itself. Job clearly marks the failure of the quest, the limits of the exercise, the realisation that the search for knowledge just leads to more questions. Experience is the mainstay of the wisdom exercise, but rather than being reliable it is experience itself that now points in a very different direction. The final theme was the personification of wisdom which is lacking in Job, except perhaps a hint in chapter 28. Von Rad compares Proverbs 8 and Job 28 and finds the latter 'gloomy and resigned: man's questioning strikes up against the impenetrable barrier of the secret and is thrown back. In Proverbs 8 on the contrary, the poem is a proclamation made by the secret of itself' ([1958] 1966b, p. 161). Yet, despite this contrast, von Rad argues that in their basic attitude the two passages are very similar. He writes:

> Wisdom, and with it participation in the secret of creation, comes to man only through obedience to the voice which ever calls him, in his actual historical situation, to decide for God. So far as we know from the Old Testament, Hebrew thought nowhere else provides so clear and rational a statement of the tension between God's universal control of the created order and his self-revelation in history. ([1958] 1966b, p. 161)

Rather than express this in salvation-history terms, as von Rad does here, I would argue that the tension is between God's control, legitimated by his acts in creation, and human attempts to comprehend the unfathomableness and power of God, the tension that is at the heart of both the figure of wisdom and of the wisdom enterprise itself.

So on all these issues there is a starting point in wisdom issues, but a decisive breaking outside its bounds. Maybe we should say that Job is wisdom plus critique. Or maybe this was the way wisdom itself developed. To test that we need to characterise the other wisdom books of Ecclesiastes, Ben Sira and the Wisdom of Solomon, as we shall go on to do. Ecclesiastes is the closest book to Job: it also criticises the wisdom exercise, but, interestingly, my finding is that it tends to restrict itself more to the mainline forms and content of wisdom than Job does.

Context

It is usually posited that the correct social context for the author of Job is a wisdom setting, since the debate takes place within the confines of a wisdom discussion and takes its starting point from there. The work may be the product of a wisdom school, but in its questioning might more naturally be the product of a dissident or group of dissidents on the fringes of a wisdom setting. We saw in Proverbs how essential a didactic context was to a definition of wisdom, whether in school or in family. Clearly, Job teaches us something, but it is not didactic in the sense of Proverbs – rather, it undermines wisdom teaching. R. N. Whybray writes on this that the basic intention of the author 'was not didactic in any strict sense' (1974, p. 62). His purpose was 'to air and discuss certain problems to which he knew of no answers, in order to provoke reflection' (p. 62). So we can probably conclude that the context in which Job was written must be one in which the wisdom tradition was known and understood, but in which there was also broader knowledge of the traditions of Israel – notably the lament and legal genres – and a definite aim to criticise traditional stances of all kinds. This was not a narrow wisdom circle, but probably represented a wider intellectual culture. We might also recall the fact that this work is not

attributed to Solomon, whereas the other so-called 'wisdom books'
are (apart from Ben Sira). This may suggest that the book was not
composed in the same circles of 'the wise' as the others, although I
do not find this a strong argument. So, while Job essentially springs
from the same intellectual and spiritual quest as other wisdom books
and must be seen as such on a broad definition, on a narrower
definition of forms, content and context, we need to have some profound reservations about simply assuming that Job is 'wisdom
literature', as narrowly defined.

Redactions

An interesting aspect of Job is that within the book itself we
find the process of toning down and reinterpretation in its various
redactions. It is in the material generally regarded as secondary or
later additions that this process first emerges. These are chiefly the
Elihu speeches, the Hymn to Wisdom and the Satan passages in
the prologue. Some would add the second Yahweh speech in Job
40:6—41:34 too, on the grounds that one is enough to make the point
and that the long description of the Behemoth and Leviathan in this
speech is of a different character from the shorter descriptions of
animals in the first speech. It is hard to see however what purpose
such an addition would have had, except to reiterate the points
already made, whereas for other additions a definite reason can be
found.

The Elihu speeches (Job 32—37) have been very differently
evaluated by scholars, some seeing them as a high point in the book
(Marshall, 1905), but others, probably the majority, finding them
repetitive both of ideas found in the speeches of the friends and the
speeches of God. In that sense they spoil the climax to come, which
is the appearance of God to Job, and on principles of plot development they could be said to have been placed badly. This, alongside
the long-winded style of the section, might suggest that it is the work
of an inferior author or redactor. If we assume that they are an
addition – largely on grounds of the non-mention of this character
in the prologue, by Job or in the epilogue, and of the presence of
angelic intermediaries which might betray the thought of a slightly
later period – what would be the purpose of it? It would chiefly

function as assisting in the strengthening of the position of the friends and possibly represent an attempt by a further author to clarify the problem of apparently innocent suffering. There is reiteration of a main theme of the speeches of the friends that God punishes only the wicked and not the righteous, that he is predictable and fair and that if people are suffering they must have sinned. Virtue is to be encouraged and vice will be punished and there is no relativising of that position. This is in direct contrast to the position of Job which stresses the arbitrariness of God. Rather than questioning God's justice, Elihu affirms it and believes in a system of fair recompense for good or evil. Suffering is then seen as a warning to the wicked to turn from that wickedness, a kind of cleansing and disciplining. Pleas to God for help do not in fact achieve anything: he may delay punishment, allowing the opportunity for repentance, and it is his right to do things in his own time. He is not to be made small by human attempts to constrain him. Does Job dare to think that he understands the ways of God? Here we link up with sentiments expressed in the Yahweh speeches.

The hymn to wisdom in chapter 28 is plausibly a separate and older piece of wisdom material put into its present position by one anxious to affirm the orthodox nature of Job as a characteristic product of wisdom circles. It is presented as a continuation of Job's speech but does not make sense on the lips of Job since it provides a different perspective, one that largely anticipates what is to come in the God speeches. It is a poem and lacks the disputational tone of the friends' speeches. It is variously regarded as a high point in the theology of the book, showing Job that there are things too wonderful for his limited understanding and as an anticipation of the climax of the work, the speeches of God, and hence an inferior addition. The likelihood of a separate context, possibly a cultic one, is a real one and the detailed description of mining may suggest authorship by one who had a close knowledge of this area of life. Rich imagery is used and the poetic quality of the hymn is high. It parallels other hymns to wisdom in Proverbs 8, Ben Sira 24 (see Chapter 8) and the Wisdom of Solomon 7:22—8:2 (see Chapter 9) and shows a similar progression from an understanding of wisdom as the domain of God to its availability to humanity in the call to fear God: 'And he said to humankind, "Truly, the fear of the Lord, that is wisdom; and to depart from evil is understanding" ' (Job 28:28).

As regards the Satan passages in the prologue, the view that they are due to later redaction is not held by the majority of scholars, but it is one that I find to be persuasive (see Batten, 1933). This view starts from the observation that there is nothing on Satan ('the Satan') in the epilogue and from the idea of this kind of dualism between God and Satan being a mainly Persian idea, and therefore slightly later. If the prologue and epilogue in some way formed an original prose story – and if this is the case, it is, in its present form, incomplete in the middle – then it seems outside the conventions of such a story (which has a folktale-like attention to detail) to leave Satan out of the ending. Neither does Satan appear in the dialogue, although, in a way, that is less surprising if the dialogue was composed separately. If we go a step further and omit the Satan passages from the original form of the story, does the story that is left make sense? I believe that it does. This would require omitting 1:6–12 and 2:1–8 so that the heavenly debate would not relativise the action in the prologue, leaving us with the initial stress on the piety of Job which relates to Ezekiel's emphasis in Ezekiel 14:14, 20. This is followed by an account of the calamities that are said to be from God, balanced in the epilogue by the restoration of children and possessions by God. We then have the patient response of Job followed, with the omission of 2:1–8, by the words of Job's wife. We then find the appearance of the three friends who at first appear merely to have the role of sitting in comforting silence, and this is balanced in the epilogue when God condemns the friends for not having 'spoken of me what is right' (Job 42:7) unlike Job. Job then offers a sacrifice acting as intercessor on their behalf. In 42:7 there is an assumption of spoken words by the friends, as found in the dialogue. The story closes with the twofold restoration of Job's fortunes – both his wealth (and hence his standing in society) and his family, albeit a new one. Interestingly, the epilogue does not mention the healing of Job's disease and this is the part in the prologue attributed to Satan. The dialogue itself does assume illness, but it is interesting that in an epilogue that in so many ways balances the prologue (for example, the exact doubling of Job's possessions at his restoration), neither Satan nor the infliction of the disease was added. We could have traces here of an original story that did not contain the Satan parts. If they were added, it is possible in my view to see them as an addition by one concerned to provide an answer to God's apparently arbitrary infliction of suffering upon Job. Along similar lines to the speeches of Elihu, it could be an orthodox attempt to redeem the situation – to try to exonerate God and affirm strict principles of justice and retribution.

The reference in the prologue to 'the Satan' would be unlikely to be from before the Persian period, thus indicating that this addition could possibly be from the fourth to the third century. As for the other secondary redactions, they may well come from the same period so that the book as a whole was substantially composed by the second century, leading to easy access to the canon. So the book is a complex whole, which probably came together over a long period; the original folk story may have come from early circles, but the main dialogue would not have been added until after the Exile. However, the final form of the book of Job is probably very different from what the author of the dialogue intended. The editorial redactors of the book contributed to this process by providing their own perspectives on the debate and their own interpretations of Job. While we have no knowledge of the contexts of these editors, it may well be that they represent a strong reaction from those maintaining a traditional world-view who nevertheless supplemented rather than replaced the original. This evidence suggests that there was a long tradition of counter-reading Job to make it acceptable. I suggest that an interpretation of Job which would no doubt have been unacceptable to the book's early interpreters but may have a great deal more to say to us today is one which focuses on the dialogue itself.

Genre – a parody?

An interesting feature of the book of Job is that varied attempts to classify it on the basis of genre have been made but no one genre classification has proved satisfactory to describe the book as a whole. Suggestions have included that it is a lament (Westermann, [1956] 1981), a legal dialogue (Richter, 1966), a tragedy (Steiner, 1979) and even a comedy, albeit a black comedy (Whedbee, 1977). While such classifications often illuminate understanding of the book by shedding light upon a particular genre to be found in parts of the text, it is usually the case that they do not work as a description of the whole book, largely because the book is made up of very varied genres. There are laments, wisdom sayings, legal genres all within its pages but none characterises the whole. Rather, the characteristic feature of the book is this diversity which has led us to have reservations about classifying Job as wisdom literature. My own suggestion is that parody, a genre that feeds on other genres, might be a suitable description of the way that the author treats the traditional genres he uses: for example, psalmic lament forms in the dialogue section are parodied so that they express the opposite of usual sentiments (Dell, 1991). I have found evidence of this technique throughout the Job dialogue, but here two examples will suffice, first that of Job 6:8–10, which is a death wish by Job in which he asks for destruction – 'O that I might have my request, and that God would grant my desire; that it would please God to crush me, that he would let loose his hand and cut me off!' (vv. 8–9) – and in so doing parodies lament forms in the Psalms that ask God for safety from attack, e.g. Psalm 55:6–8: 'And I say, O that I had wings like a dove! I would fly away and be at rest.' Second, there is Job 7:17–18 which parodies Psalm 8:4. The psalmist expresses awe at the favour God shows to human beings in his creation: 'What are human beings that you are mindful of them, mortals that you care for them?' Job however turns this sentiment around when he complains, 'What are human beings, that you make so much of them, that you set your mind on them, visit them every morning, test them every moment?' For Job, God's concern for humans is oppressive – he longs to get away from God's attention.

B. Zuckerman also uses the genre of parody as a description of the genre of Job, although he uses it to describe the nature of the overall structure of the book, with its disjunctions and contradictions. He describes the relationship of what he calls the poem of Job to the legend of Job as a 'contrapuntal relationship between a parody and its conventional tradition' (1991, p. 47). He finds the author replacing 'Job the silent' with 'Job the verbose' in the dialogue and subverting the conventions of traditional dialogue and appeal forms from the ancient Near East, and he finds in Job a counter-deity theme and parodistic preoccupation with death balancing resurrection themes in the prologue. Whilst I find unpalatable Zuckerman's ideas about a counter-deity and resurrection themes in the prologue, he has pointed to the wider implications of the use of parody in Job. In my study I looked at the way the author of the dialogue, in many passages, parodied items of the Israelite tradition to stage his protest, whereas Zuckerman's concern is with the overall structure of the book. In fact, the combination of our studies strengthens the argument for seeing the author of Job as having deliberately used genres known to him in a subversive manner in order to counter traditional ideas of his day. One might ask: is parody not then just another suggestion for an overall genre to add to the list? Why should this be any more convincing than other suggestions? My response would be that in fact parody is not a genre like others. It is a parasitic genre which makes use of any other genre for its own purpose and can thus accommodate a diversity of genres within its range. Its purpose is the deliberate improper use of an existing genre, a sending up of the original genre.

In the light of such findings, the dialogue section comes into prominence rather than the 'story' in the prologue and epilogue that has tended to be the focus of attention in Jewish and Christian interpretation of the book (Besserman, 1979). We read in the Epistle of James of the 'endurance of Job' (James 5:11) and he has often been portrayed as a paradigm of the uncomplaining sufferer – a picture far from the truth when one focuses on the dialogue section of Job. Recent scholarship is interested in how the book has been interpreted from early times and the history of Job illustration has been examined by S. Terrien (1996). There is an accompanying interest in readers of all types and in how the subjectivity of any reader's situation might affect a reading of a book such as Job (Clines, 1989; Good, 1990). Also, particular readings of Job from fresh perspectives have led to exciting new ideas – from psychologists (Schlobin, 1992), liberationists (Gutiérrez, 1987) and feminists (van Wolde 1997; Brenner, 1989), for example. However, there is much work continuing on the more objective side in literary-critical, theological, sociological and other areas and it seems that new insights on the book are far from being in short supply.

4: ECCLESIASTES/QOHELETH

And I applied my mind to know wisdom and to know madness and folly. I perceived that this also is but a chasing after wind. (Eccl. 1.16).

The book of Ecclesiastes, otherwise known as Qoheleth, is, like Job, a questioning work, but in many ways it has more in common with Proverbs in its aphoristic style and instructional tone. Interestingly, both Proverbs and Ecclesiastes are attributed, if indirectly, to Solomon, and Job is not, although in fact Qoheleth, the Preacher (from the verb *qhl*, to assemble, gather), may be an indication of the name of the author of this book, a teacher who takes on the guise of Solomon for didactic purposes (1:1, 12–18). It is a work that is a more or less self-contained literary whole, like Job, although the presence of contradictions has led scholars to put forward complex theories about structure, purpose and redactions. Such interests are not confined to modern scholars either – exploration into the concerns of pre-critical interpreters of Ecclesiastes (Murphy, 1992; Dell, 1994b) has revealed their concern with the contradictions in the book, which were a barrier to canonisation until they were harmonised with Torah.

Historical concerns

Most scholars agree that this is a post-exilic work, probably slightly later than Job, both on grounds of language (Fredericks, 1988) and critique of earlier proverbial material, although we may wish to dissociate ourselves from strictly developmental models that see one book as a development of another. C. L. Seow (1997) has recently made the point that one cannot interpret Qoheleth solely as a reaction to practical texts such as Proverbs since one cannot be certain about the precise chronological development of each. However, in the critique of the world-view represented in Proverbs and quotation of proverbs that represent it, Qoheleth is clearly standing at a later point in the wisdom tradition. Recent scholarship has dated the book in the Persian period (Seow, 1997) on socio-economic grounds accompanied by appeal to epigraphic finds and the results of archaeological excavations. However, majority opinion favours the early Greek period, finding similar socio-economic reasons for placing the book in third-century Judaea. It is possible that there is influence on the book from Greek thought, although this is very much a matter of debate. This view depends upon positing the Hellenisation of cultured, educated Jews as starting quite early in the Ptolomaic period, upon finding the influence of Greek language on phrases in the book, and, most significantly, upon finding the influence of certain Greek philosophies in the thought of the book. Although older scholars found extensive influence from Greek philosophy, it has been recognised that no one philosophical system fits Qoheleth's thought exactly and that each system has aspects that certainly do not fit in. R. Braun (1973) has recently claimed that it is a kind of pessimistic Greek popular philosophy that Qoheleth espoused rather than a formal system. This may not indicate dependence upon any particular work, but rather a wider influence from the Hellenistic thought-world beginning to infiltrate Jewish culture. Some scholars (e.g. Whitley, 1979) have dated Ecclesiastes later – into the second century BC – and have found extensive influence upon his thought from Epicureanism and Stoicism. However, majority opinion places the book in the third century BC. It cannot come from much later than this as it was clearly known to the author of Eccesiasticus or Ben Sira who wrote in c. 180 BC. It would probably be wrong to deny any Greek influence upon Qoheleth – the distinctive style of his work probably indicates this – but we might fall short of positing any strong dependence on formal systems of Greek philosophy.

Literary-critical concerns

The book contains contradictions of sentiment which have led some to scour it for later additions. However, this is generally regarded as largely unnecessary among recent scholars. Those such as J. A. Loader, for example, have seen the contradictions as deliberate juxtaposition of opposite ideas on the part of the author. Such 'polar' structures are described by Loader as 'patterns of tension created by the counterposition of two elements to one another' (1979, p. 1). He sees Ecclesiastes as made of up a number of well-structured units of which the forms are the framework within which the content or 'thought-structures' function. The author is regarded as constantly counterpoising poles to each other and creating tension by their opposition. Opposing themes such as 'toil and joy' (9:3–7), 'talk and silence' (5:2–7), 'the worth and worthlessness of wisdom' (1:12—2:26) are discussed by the author in passages structured in such a way as to highlight the tension. Loader argues that polar structures in Qoheleth are fundamental, occurring in almost every passage of the book.

There may also have been a redactional stage as well to which the epilogue can be attributed. This last part of the book (12:9–14) is often agreed to be an addition, and in fact some recent scholars (notably Fox, 1977) have seen the framework (1:1–2 and 12:9f.) as the work of the main author and the rest as earlier material quoted by this author (see also recently Christianson, 1998). Others (Shead, 1996; Vogels, 1995) find the book to be essentially a unity, Shead arguing that redactors imitated the style of the original so as to create an overall feeling of unity, and Vogels arguing that the epilogue forms the climax and conclusion of the work. This view tends towards the kind of final-form readings we found to be popular in recent studies of Job and depends on a reading that regards the epilogue as consistent with the thought of the rest of the book. It ignores the fact that the epilogue makes fresh theological connections, notably that between the fear of God and keeping his commandments, in line with a developing interest in the law (Dell, 1994b), which reflects upon the wisdom exercise in a way uncharacteristic of the rest of the book and is somewhat vague as to the content of the book, describing the Preacher as seeking 'to find pleasing words' (Eccl. 12:10).

Theological content and mood

Let us consider now the theological content and mood of the book. The author in apparently cynical vein uses various methods to question traditional wisdom teachings. Like the author of Job, he appeals to experience, but his own experience contradicts traditional wisdom, hence his citation of proverbial material with his own interpretation added (see below). He appeals to the order of nature, but only to compare its permanence with the transience of human life (e.g. Eccl. 3:11–22). He recognises the difference between the righteous and the wicked and finds that they meet the same fate, for example Ecclesiastes 8:14: 'There is a vanity that takes place on earth, that there are righteous people who are treated according to the conduct of the wicked, and there are wicked people who are treated according to the conduct of the righteous. I said that this also is vanity.' He looks for success in life, and finds that it is an empty thing (Eccl. 2:4–11). The phrase that keeps making an appearance is 'all is vanity and a striving after wind' (Eccl. 1:14). The book opens with a demonstration of the vanity of human effort, which it characterises as toil or labour (Eccl. 1:3: 'What do people gain from all the toil at which they toil under the sun?'). Then it shows the futility of attempting to find meaning in past events or to reflect on what lies in the future (Eccl. 1:9–11: 'What has been is what will be, and what has been done is what will be done; there is nothing new under the sun' (v. 9)). Things happen in their appointed time, and although this can be observed, it cannot be understood or predicted (3:1–5). Justice is a vain pursuit, as is wealth (Eccl. 3:9–17; 4:10–11, 13–14). This is followed by observations on unpunished wickedness (e.g. Eccl. 4:1) and on the fact that all people share the same fate which is death (e.g. Eccl. 3:20). According to Qoheleth, there is an order in the universe but humans cannot comprehend it and so cannot achieve any security, either material or spiritual (e.g. Eccl. 11:5). Reason and observation demonstrate no sense in human life, and so his best advice is to enjoy life (e.g. Eccl. 11:9–10). This is a far cry from the optimism of the book of Proverbs. There is a God and a need to fear him, but God is ultimately unknowable. Furthermore, the wisdom exercise has its limitations; this wisdom, if it can be called wisdom, looks at the world but finds very different answers. It approaches reality with a realism that is frightening.

So the author of Ecclesiastes is generally seen as pessimistic in the extreme, having given up the possibility of a meaningful relationship with God and advocating a resigned cynicism about life – although there have been some interesting alternative suggestions, for example that of R. N. Whybray (1982) who has argued that he was a preacher of joy. He draws attention to the fact that, although the negative sentiments I have just outlined are there, giving an overall air of resignation to the book, there are also to be found some more positive sentiments such as the enjoyment of life. Just because all is vanity, one might as well 'eat, drink and be merry' for tomorrow one may die. Furthermore, this enjoyment is seen as a gift of God – it is not a hedonism born of despair. He finds positive the fact that, despite an emphasis on God's order which humans cannot comprehend, the author does not give up on practical advice to human beings for good living and so demonstrates a belief that God's intentions might be influenced by human actions. He finds positive thoughts among the author's seeming preoccupation with death; his view of death as a waste compels him to advocate valuing the gift of life now, not waiting until you are too old and grey to enjoy it. The author of Ecclesiastes quotes the proverb 'a living dog is better than a dead lion' (Eccl. 9:4) to make the point that life is generally to be preferred to death and where there's life there's hope. On the other hand, there are one or two cases where death might be a release, for those for example who are subjected to cruelty and oppression all their lives (Eccl. 4:1–3), for those who cannot enjoy their wealth (Eccl. 6:1–6), and for those who have no hope at all. Wealth and toil, both of which the author sees as vain pursuits, can be seen, claims Whybray, as having their rightful place in the context of a proper relationship with God. This is the cause for joy: that God gives many gifts to humankind in which we can rejoice even if we do not fully understand them. Even divine justice, which seems at times to be arbitrary, at other times appears to be working according to the old principles advocated in Proverbs of good things for the righteous, calamity for the wicked.

What Whybray has drawn attention to here is the contradiction and tension in the thought of Ecclesiastes which makes it open to interpretation in various ways (cf. also Gordis, 1939–40; Good, 1965; Johnston, 1976). His reading enables us to see Ecclesiastes in closer relationship to the book of Proverbs in that the citation of traditional ideas is not only in the context of a negative refutation. Furthermore, in calling his readers to enjoy life and in acknowledgement of God's gifts, Qoheleth is balancing his more negative sentiments concerning the failure of humans to master life and control their own destiny.

Recently, J. T. Walsh (1982) has characterised the mood of Qoheleth as 'peaceful despair', whilst E. Levine (1997) describes it as 'serious humour' to teach others to cope with the uncertainties of life. It is clear that there is a cynical note in the book, and yet one that is balanced by a pragmatic stance. The tension between God-given wisdom and human acquisition of it is brought out in the book, in a similar manner to Job but without the anguished despair of that book. The word *hebel*, vanity, which appears 38 times in the book is a kind of keyword in the light of which all things are relativised. The message is to enjoy life whilst you can (2:24) but in the recognition that all things are relativised by death, the great leveller (2:16–18; 5:15). God holds the key to events, but the real meaning is hidden from us (3:1–2). The best thing to do is to fear God (3:14; 5:7; 7:18; 8:12–13) or to go one stage further, as the epilogue asserts, and both fear God and keep his commandments. We will now turn to a consideration of Ecclesiastes as wisdom literature.

Form

When we look at forms in Ecclesiastes we find that the smaller genres that make up the book are mainly from the wisdom tradition (e.g. 7:1–12; 9:17f.) and not predominantly from other areas of life. The first form which we shall look for is the proverb. This we find sometimes in a series, as in chapter 7:1–13 and in chapter 10, but also in isolation, for example Ecclesiastes 1:14 with accompanying interpretation: 'The wise have eyes in their head, but fools walk in darkness. Yet I perceived that the same fate befalls all of them.' It is not certain whether these proverbs were all pre-existent within the tradition or whether some were composed by Qoheleth with the purpose of refutation. Both possibilities are likely and the two techniques of quotation and composition are not mutually incompatible. R. N. Whybray (1981) suggests criteria by which to identify quotations from outside sources rather than those which are a foil for Qoheleth's own teaching and isolates the following verses as likely to be such quotations: Ecclesiastes 2:14a; 4:5; 4:6; 7:6a; 9:17; 10:2; 10:12. The proverbs in which the author states his own view are likely to be his own compositions while the ones apparently quoted may be genuine quotations or at least restatements by the author of conventional ideas. The epilogue suggests that there were more proverbs that the author might have used (Eccl. 12:9, 11). One of the major collections of proverbs is found in chapter 10. The chapter begins with proverbs about dead flies spoiling the perfumer's ointment and continues with a miscellany of subjects close to the wisdom writer's heart: contrasting the wise man and the fool; sayings about accidents that may befall those who are too eager; and words about using one's wisdom wisely rather than foolishly. We find in 10:12–14 proverbs about communication, again in connection with the wise man and the fool – a familiar theme from the book of Proverbs. One of Qoheleth's techniques is to throw up a deliberate contrast between two proverbs which highlight the tension between different experiential formulations of truth (e.g. Eccl. 4:5–6: 'Fools fold their hands and consume their own flesh. Better is a handful with quiet than two handfuls with toil, and a chasing after wind').

A second main smaller genre of wisdom is the instruction which may be likened to the instructions of Proverbs 1—9. This is the personal input of the author and errs on the positive side of Qoheleth's thought, for example the instruction to enjoy life in Ecclesiastes 9:7–10. Another instruction motif is found in chapter 10 and concerns behaviour towards a ruler which here takes the form of a prohibition (v. 4: 'If the anger of the ruler rises against you, do not leave your post, for calmness will undo great offences'), commands and prohibitions being a part of the traditional wisdom repertoire. This theme links up with instruction at the beginning of chapter 8 concerning conduct before a king. There is also a thematic link with the 'example story' about a king and a poor wise man found at the end of chapter 9, this kind of moral tale being another common wisdom genre. The poem on old age in chapter 12 is often likened to the Egyptian Instruction of Ptahhotep which opens with a comparable poem (see Chapter 7). We do not find the form of the hymn to wisdom in Ecclesiastes; however, the long didactic poems in the book in Ecclesiastes 1:4–9 and 3:2–8 come closest to this form.

When the author wants to make some relativising comment of his own, which is usually on the pessimistic side, he uses a third main smaller genre, that of 'reflection'. We might liken this to the autobiographical narrative form found in Proverbs, although it clearly goes well beyond the confines of that form, or we might liken it to the 'royal testament' form found in Egypt (see Chapter 7). The genre of reflection is by far the most dominant in the book and is a particular characteristic of this author, giving the book its personal flavour. Part of this individuality is the use of refrains for emphasis, in particular the refrain that 'all is vanity and a striving after wind', but also favourite words such as 'under the sun', 'toil', 'gain' and 'gift of God'. However, the most important characteristic of the reflection is that it incorporates within itself several subgenres such as sayings, proverbs, rhetorical questions and quotations, and the didactic poems, all from the wisdom tradition – in fact, it feeds off these other genres. Thus in chapter 10 the reflection comes in verses 5–7 which has the effect of relativising the preceding and succeeding wisdom sayings. Here we find a remark about the overturning of the usual social order which introduces a note of uncertainty, thus providing a context for the proverbs that follow.

This genre 'reflection' both includes traditional wisdom elements and provides room for Qoheleth's own remarks. He uses wisdom subgenres in the context of a reflection section in order to contradict their assertions; for example Ecclesiastes 8:12–13 is negated by the framework in verses 11–14. This pattern is termed by Gordis the 'use of quotations' technique. He finds four methods of quotation in Ecclesiastes. The author may quote a proverb to back up an argument (e.g. Eccl. 10:18; 11:1–2) or he may use part of a proverb to support an argument, only citing the rest for the sake of completeness (e.g. Eccl. 5:1–2; 11:3–4). He might use a proverb to provide a starting point for further commentary (e.g. Eccl. 7:1–14; 4:9–12; 5:9–12; 8:2–4). Finally, he may make use of contrasting pro-verbs juxtaposed to each other (e.g. Eccl. 4:5–6; 9:16–18). Elsewhere, Qoheleth narrates a tale or 'example' story (e.g. Eccl. 4:13–16; 9:13–16) using the traditional form within his own argument.

I have already mentioned the work of J. A. Loader who describes the originality of the author in the context of exploring polar structures in which traditional forms are used in a fresh context – he 'takes over current forms to serve his own purpose' (1979,

p. 115). He demonstrates how many of the typical literary forms to be found in wisdom literature are used in the book but as part of new structural units, for example Ecclesiastes 11:1–6. He argues that a polar tension may be found in the book between the use of typical forms from wisdom literature and the use of literary units peculiar to Qoheleth, such as the reflection. I have elsewhere characterised this as a 'reuse of forms' on the part of the author – taking traditional forms with their usual content and placing them in a fresh context that relativises them (Dell, 1991). We can conclude on form therefore that the author of Ecclesiastes uses forms predominantly from the wisdom tradition but uses his own instructions and reflections to convey a personal message.

Content

In the realm of content, the author of Ecclesiastes is concerned, like the authors of Proverbs, with the quest for meaning. However, it takes a very different form, and so we may find some difficulty matching the content of Ecclesiastes with that which we found in Proverbs to characterise wisdom literature. His starting point is an exploration using the concepts of wisdom (Eccl. 7:23–9) but he finds the exercise to be bankrupt. The contradictions of thought in the book, which we have seen are largely due to quotation of traditional ideas, give the book an occasionally optimistic note and seem to anchor the book in the wisdom tradition. However, within the context of the whole book we find a questioning and unorthodoxy that leaves no stone unturned in the challenging of accepted values.

The first theme of order in the world is presented in a very different way here. The author lacks trust in human ability to discover the deep things of God (Eccl. 7:24). All knowledge is in the realm of God and comes from him (Eccl. 2:16). There is an order and a rational rule which belongs to the sphere of God (Eccl. 2:11) – that is made clear in the poem in Ecclesiastes 3:2–11. However, human beings lack the ability to find it out (Eccl. 1:13), and here it is made clear that the author does not have confidence in the wisdom tradition's reliance on knowledge gained from experience. Rather, he cites examples of that accumulated wisdom – examples that are often contradictory – and then shows how personal experience often undermines such truisms and that simple proverbs do not satisfy a deeper questioning. Ironically, human beings yearn for knowledge and an understanding of these mysteries (Eccl. 1:18). Yet, they cannot secure their future in the manner of the 'act–consequence relationship' promoted by Proverbs because God's activity is unpredicable and ultimately unknowable (Eccl. 11:5). Human beings are as likely to miss meaningful events as to be aware of them since they have not got the knowledge to match deed to occasion (Eccl. 7:23–9). He uses the example story in Ecclesiastes 9:13–16 of a poor wise man whose knowledge goes to waste because no one remembers him when the city is threatened and calamity strikes.

The second theme of the ambiguity of events and the meaning of life is also pursued in Ecclesiastes. Here contradiction points to ambiguity and the unknowability of God's activity is a barrier to a deep understanding of life. There is ambiguity in the sentiment that the human lot is on the one hand determined by God but on the other corrupted by human beings themselves (Eccl. 7:29: 'See, this alone I found, that God made human beings straight-forward, but they have devised many schemes'). The more usual idea is that God has determined the times for major events in life and for all human activities (Eccl. 3:2–11), but human beings do not have access to that knowledge (Eccl. 11:5) and hence it becomes meaningless. His attempt to discover meaning in life ultimately leads Qoheleth only to muse on death and how death comes alike to wise and foolish (Eccl. 2:14). He tests various attempts to find meaning in life, for example fasting, toil, possessions, fame and knowledge, and denies them absolute value. He also airs the absurdity that time eventually erodes the memory of human achievements (Eccl. 2:16: 'For there is no enduring remembrance of the wise or of fools, seeing that in the days to come all will have been long forgotten. How can the wise die just like fools?'). Yet, there is a sense of acceptance of life as it comes and even a concession that some attempts to find meaning do possess a fleeting significance, such as the pleasure of eating and drinking and finding enjoyment in work (Eccl. 2:24; 7:14; 8:15).

The third theme we found to be central is that of punishment and reward. In Ecclesiastes the loss of trust in God's just and individual accounting on the basis of individual human behaviour leads to a questioning of the righteousness of God himself (Eccl. 8:17). There is no confidence as to whether God will reward righteous behaviour or punish the wicked (Eccl. 9:1–2). Experience suggests that the opposite is so often the case – that the wicked prosper and the good are punished (Eccl. 7:15; 8:14 – although we find this contradicted in 3:17 and 8:13), and hence God appears to be indifferent to human conduct. Furthermore, death as the great equaliser makes a mockery of strenuous attempts to lead an upright life (Eccl. 7:16).

The fourth theme was life as the supreme good, a theme that is sometimes affirmed (Eccl. 7:17–18; 9:4–6) but often denied in the light of death which brings rest from labour (Eccl. 6:4–5; 4:1–4). There is no thought of suicide and this omission adds weight to the argument that for Qoheleth, although he verges on despair at times, life is still ultimately the supreme good and 'there is nothing better for people under the sun than to eat, and drink, and enjoy themselves' (Eccl. 8:15).

A fifth concern, which can be termed confidence in wisdom, is a theme of Proverbs that is severely questioned in Ecclesiastes. Nevertheless, wisdom is his starting point and at times there is a positive attitude towards it – for example the idea that it is a prize to be gained and a protection and security (Eccl. 2:26; 7:11, 19). Also in chapter 7, however, he does not advise trying too hard to be wise. In Ecclesiastes 8:1 we read, 'Wisdom makes one's face shine and the hardness of one's countenance is changed', but then later in chapter 8, 'However much they may toil in seeking, they will not find it out' (Eccl. 8:17). Qoheleth sometimes sees the exercise of wisdom as pointless in the light of death, and particularly in the light of the fact that the fruits of one's own toil are often not enjoyed by oneself but by those who come after who did not toil for it (Eccl. 2:18–21). This relates to the emphasis on the inaccessibility of knowledge described above. There is clearly a good deal of vacillating here on the part of the author between a positive and a negative assessment of wisdom, and this is possibly a deliberate tension designed to bring out the contradictions.

The final theme of the personification of wisdom is lacking

in Ecclesiastes, although the personal flavour to the book is reminiscent of the personal call of wisdom in Proverbs 1—9. Thus we find a contradictory content in Ecclesiastes – a sharp questioning counterbalanced by citation of opposite sentiments – that brings out the relativity of life, the ambiguities of the quest for wisdom, the search for the knowledge of God, and so on. The content is at home within wisdom circles despite the critique that is applied. So, in terms of content, we find in Ecclesiastes a sharp questioning of the tradition and yet one counterbalanced by quotation from the tradition and contradiction of thought in a number of areas.

Context

Let us turn now to the question of context. Early Jewish and Christian tradition attributed the work to Solomon. According to Jewish tradition, he was supposed to have written the Song of Songs in his youth, Proverbs in middle age and Ecclesiastes in old age. Although this Jewish tradition is first and foremost interested in the character of Solomon and in the events of his life, it is interesting that the mood of the book is one of resignation that would seem to belong more naturally to one mature in years; we also have the poem about old age in chapter 12 which might suggest personal experience of the ageing process. It has been thought that Solomonic attribution is one of the main reasons for ascribing the book to the wisdom category although it may be less important than it at first appears. Furthermore, the Song of Songs is rarely included in the wisdom category despite these grounds. The persona of Solomon lends a certain authority to the book – was this a later interpolation to enhance the authority of the book on the part of a redactor, or was the Solomonic guise a deliberate motif adopted by Qoheleth? The latter option seems the more likely, given the extended royal auto-biography section in 1:12–18. E. Christianson (1998) has recently argued that the Solomonic guise can be seen to characterise the main text throughout rather than being confined to the first two chapters, regarding sympathy with the poor as a not inappropriate concern for a king, and regarding the reference to 'one woman in a thousand' in 7:28 as to the many wives and concubines of King Solomon.

Luther ([1536] 1972) suggested that contradictions in Qoheleth's thought were explicable by imagining Solomon in dialogue with political associates. This same idea has resurfaced in R. Gordis' idea of quotations (1939–40) and T. A. Perry's idea that two points of view are represented in the book (1993). This idea of dialogue in which thesis is met with antithesis, in which experience encounters faith and in which two voices are heard in dialogue, is in many ways an attractive one and gets across a sense of the tensions contained in the book. It accounts for the unusual style of the book in its use of traditional wisdom and extensive critique of it, it draws out the tensions that characterise the content such as the call to enjoy life which is in tension with death as the great relativiser, and it suggests a teaching or preaching context in which ideas are cited, tested and examined. The theological aspect to the book may suggest a broader temple school-type context rather than a more secular educational one. The epilogue describes Qoheleth as arranging proverbs with great care, which suggests a man steeped in the proverbial tradition. Yet, Qoheleth, the 'assembler' of the people, could also be seen as assembling the evidence for the case against traditional wisdom from within the tradition itself.

It would seem fair to conclude from this discussion that Ecclesiastes is to be regarded as mainstream wisdom, a book that uses forms and ideas from within that tradition. In using almost exclusively wisdom forms, the author of Ecclesiastes remains much closer to mainline wisdom than the author of Job does. Ecclesiastes stands at a later stage of the biblical wisdom tradition and uses the characteristic forms and content of that tradition in order to criticise it. Ecclesiastes therefore represents a protesting or sceptical strain which arises closely out of the wisdom exercise and so should be characterised as mainline wisdom literature, if of a deeply questioning kind. M. V. Fox (1988) has recently argued that, although Qoheleth goes beyond the knowledge of received wisdom to create knowledge of his own, he regards it as essentially in line with existing wisdom. It is clear that the author is working from within the wisdom tradition, testing its maxims against his own experience. His sentiments are anti-wisdom in that they stress the futility of being able to know anything with certainty, and yet the God-given aspect of the wisdom quest is confirmed. There is a realism about the human quest for wisdom which then links up with a more religious world-view which recommends simply trusting in God without having any answers (3:11), an outlook which is expanded upon in the epilogue.

Outside influences on the book

The book of Ecclesiastes also shows the influence of a thought-world beyond strictly wisdom circles. A number of parallels have been noted by C. C. Forman (1960) between Ecclesiastes and Genesis 1—11. For example, the idea of humans being made of dust and returning to dust (Eccl. 3:20; 12:7; cf. Gen. 2:7; 3:19); the propensity to sin (Eccl. 7:20; 7:29; 8:11; 9:3; c.f. Gen. 2:9—3:14); the need for companionship (Eccl. 4:9–12; 9:9; Gen. 1:27; 2:18f); the limitations on human knowledge (Eccl. 1:13; 8:7; 10:14b; Gen. 2:15f; 11:6f); the idea of life as toil (Eccl. 1:3; 2:22; Gen. 2:15; 3:14–19); a preoccupation with death (Eccl. 3:20; 9:4–6; 11:8; 12:7; Gen. 2:17; 3:3f, 19–24; 6:13); and the idea that God is sovereign (Eccl. 3:10—14; 5:7, Gen. 1:28–30; 3:5, 22; 6:6). There is also a link with Genesis in ideas of the order and regularity of nature (Eccl. 3:11–12; Gen. 8:21f) and of life being essentially 'good' (Eccl. 2:24; Gen. 1). W. Zimmerli (1980) thought that Qoheleth deliberately refers to the creation account in order to refute the traditional use made of it at his time. Others such as R. K. Johnston (1976) argue that Qoheleth is calling the wisdom tradition back to its central focus on the art of steering a successful path in life in which the creation and order motifs have an essential role.

Another scholar (Gordis, 1962), as well as noting the parallels with Genesis 1—11, finds influence from Deuteronomy, 1 Samuel and 1 Kings. For example, Ecclesiastes 3:14, in its idea of being unable to add or subtract from the word of God, recalls Deuteronomy 4:2 and 13:1, and the passage on vows in Ecclesiastes 5:3f recalls Deuteronomy 23:22. It is possible that Ecclesiastes 5:5 contains an overtone of Leviticus 5:4. Ecclesiastes 7:20 recalls a passage in the prayer of Solomon in 1 Kings 8:46, and Ecclesiastes 4:17b resembles 1 Samuel 15:22. The author of Ecclesiastes therefore reuses forms from within wisdom for his own purposes but also recalls passages from a broader range of texts, passages that would have been familiar to his hearers perhaps. In this he is standing in an intellectual tradition that is beginning to open out, as it goes on to do more overtly in Sirach and the Wisdom of Solomon with specific linkage with the legal traditions of Israel.

5: WISDOM PSALMS

The mouths of the righteous utter wisdom and their tongues speak justice. (Psalm 37:30).

The definition of wisdom is a vexed question in itself, but none more so than when applied to the ill-defined category of wisdom psalms. Yet as D. F. Morgan remarks, 'There is, perhaps, no collection of writings outside the wisdom literature itself which contains so much evidence of wisdom literary forms and teachings as the Psalms' (1981, p. 125). This suggests that, while complex, the task of tackling this category is a worthwhile one. If we apply our criteria of form, content and context we find that many psalms contain wisdom forms, some wisdom content and some may have been devised or at least edited in wisdom circles. This has the effect of a grading of wisdom psalms: some, such as Psalms 37, 49 and 73, are clearly contenders, while others, such as Psalms 19, 25 and 32, are on the edge of the category. The classification tends to be made on the basis of affinities with more well-established wisdom books. As J. Day remarks, the problem is 'how many wisdom characteristics a psalm must possess before it may legitimately be so described [as a wisdom psalm]' (1994, pp. 54–5).

The full range of psalms that have been suggested to belong in whole or in part to the wisdom category is as follows: Psalms 1, 14, 19, 25, 32, 33, 34, 36, 37, 39, 49, 51, 53, 62, 73, 78, 90, 92, 94, 104, 105, 106, 111, 112, 119, 127, 128. On seeing this number of psalms selected for this group, we might well question whether we need a category 'wisdom psalms' at all. R. N. Whybray has recently argued that the separation of the category 'wisdom psalms' from the rest of the Psalter is forced and that the category itself is a misleading one. He writes: 'It may be concluded that the use of "wisdom psalms" as a blanket term for all those psalms in the Psalter which express serious thoughts on religious matters as distinct from spontaneous expressions of faith, confession, praise, distress etc. is a mistaken one' (1995, p. 160). He notes that its use tends to weaken the distinctiveness of the notion of 'wisdom' in Old Testament studies and detracts from a full appreciation of the character of the whole Psalter. It is certainly true that the Psalter would not be a suitable starting point for attempting to characterise what wisdom is, nor would it be easy, given the mixing of types within the Psalter, to sideline the wisdom psalms as a separate category with little or no contact with the rest. However, I would contend that it is helpful to assess the nature of some psalms using the wisdom criteria of form, content and context that we have already discussed in previous chapters. We will see that wisdom is really inseparable from other genres of Old Testament material in the Psalter, and that all we can really speak of is a general wisdom influence. Let us turn, then, to our criteria of form, content and context.

Form

One problem with ranging wisdom psalms together on the basis of form is that the wisdom grouping is not really a form-critical category because the links tend to be more thematic than formal. There are some wisdom forms, but few whole psalms can be designated wisdom on the basis of form alone. E. Gerstenberger (1974), in an article on form-critical approaches as applied to the psalms, uses the criteria of form that we have used ourselves to test for wisdom influence. He writes: 'formulaic expressions and form elements quite common in wisdom writings reappear in some psalms' (p. 219).

Examples of these forms are proverbs, for example Psalm 1:6 which provides a summarising contrast between the righteous and the wicked: 'For the Lord watches over the way of the righteous, but the way of the wicked will perish.' Other examples include Psalm 33:16–17, which builds on an idea rather than providing a contrast: 'A king is not saved by his great army; a warrior is not delivered by his great strength. The war horse is a vain hope for victory, and by its great might it cannot save.' Further examples are Psalms 34:7, 10, 22; 37:2, 8–9, 12–13, 21. Psalm 37:12–13 contains a contrast: 'The wicked plot against the righteous, and gnash their teeth at them; but the Lord laughs at the wicked, for he sees that their day is coming.' This is followed in verse 16 by a 'better than' saying: 'Better is a little that the righteous has than the abundance of many wicked', cf. Proverbs 15:16: 'Better is a little with the fear of the Lord than great treasure and trouble with it.' Psalm 127 is mainly made up of a series of proverbs that contain themes and images from the wisdom corpus.

Another form that we find in the wisdom psalms is the numerical saying, for example Psalm 62:11: 'Once God has spoken; twice have I heard this . . .' We also find lists, for example Psalm 104:14f, which lists God's acts in creation. There are also rhetorical questions, for example Psalm 49:5–6: 'Why should I fear in times of trouble, when the iniquity of my persecutors surrounds me, those who trust in their wealth and boast of the abundance of their riches?' There are exhortations in didactic tone, such as Psalm 34:14: 'Depart from evil, and do good; seek peace and pursue it' (cf. Psalms 62:10; 94:9–11). There is the 'Happy is . . .' formula that has a place in both liturgical and educational use, to be found in the opening to Psalm 1: 'Happy are those who do not follow the advice of the wicked . . .', and in Psalms 32:1, 33:12, 128:1. We recall the use of this formula in Proverbs 3:13; 8:32, 34; 14:21; 16:20; 20:7; 28:14 and 29:8.

There is material of the instruction genre in a number of psalms which is often made up of various smaller genre elements as outlined above. One example is Psalm 14:1–3 which opens with a didactic description of the godless with God looking down from heaven to see if there are any who are wise, followed by rhetorical question and exhortation in verses 4–5. Also Psalm 32:8–9 contains wisdom instruction: 'I will instruct you and teach you the way you should go; I will counsel you with my eye upon you. Do not be like a horse or a mule, without understanding, whose temper must be curbed with bit and bridle, else it will not stay near you.' The reference to walking in the way – the idea of life as a path is a popular one in Proverbs – and the use of an illustration from nature are both reminiscent of the wisdom approach. Also Psalm 34 contains exhortations in verses 8–9 resembling the Instruction form found in Proverbs 1—9 (e.g. Prov. 4:1) and also some proverbs in vv. 7, 10 and 22. It is usually only the second part of this psalm that is seen as a strong contender for the wisdom category since it contains most of the wisdom elements, although the whole is an acrostic which might suggest that it was composed as a unity. Verse 11 contains a wisdom formula, 'Come, O children, listen to me . . .' (cf. Prov. 4:1; 5:7; 7:24; 8:32), followed by mention of educational intent (v. 11b), rhetorical question (v. 12), instruction in exhortatory tone (vv. 13–14) and differentiation between the righteous and the wicked (vv. 15–22). Psalm 36:1–4 contains a description of the evildoer that may have derived from wisdom instruction and this is framed at the end of the psalm by a contrast with the righteous. Psalm 49 has an imposing 'teacher's summons' at the beginning which indicates a wisdom psalm, while also suggesting a liturgical context in the sentiment, 'I will incline my ear to a proverb; I will solve my riddle to the music of the harp' (v. 1). There is a refrain which appears in verses 12 and 20 which is proverbial in form. Psalm 78 too has an opening summons that recalls the wisdom tradition: 'Give ear, O my people, to my teaching; incline your ears to the words of my mouth' (v. 1), although the rest of the psalm is generally not categorised as a wisdom psalm.

Another important form in Proverbs was the autobiographical narrative. There is a small amount of autobiographical narrative in Psalms 37 and 73. In 37:25, 35 (cf. Prov. 24:30–2; 30:7–9; Eccl. 2) we read: 'I have been young, and now am old, yet I have not seen the righteous forsaken or their children begging bread' (v. 25), and then, by contrast, 'I have seen the wicked oppressing, and towering like a cedar of Lebanon' (v. 35). In Psalm 73:15–17 we find a similar first-person narrative: 'If I had said, I will talk on in this way, I would have been untrue to the circle of your children. But when I thought how to understand this, it seemed to me a wearisome task, until I went into the sanctuary of God; then I perceived their end.'

We do not find wisdom poems to personified wisdom such as appear in Proverbs. There are furthermore some forms that are on the edge of the wisdom category. One is hymnic passages, as in Psalm 19 which contains a hymn to the Creator (vv. 1–6) followed by a meditation on the Torah (vv. 7–14), a note of instruction being found in verse 11 and some of the language of wisdom being found in the section on the Torah. The hymn to creation genre is reminiscent of ancient Near Eastern hymns to the sun god, especially those from Egypt (see Steck, 1980). However, the close relation of wisdom and Torah in this psalm has led scholars (e.g. Crenshaw,

1982) to classify it as a 'torah meditation' psalm rather than as 'wisdom'. Another is the alphabetic acrostic in which each verse begins with a consecutive letter of the Hebrew alphabet, such as is found in Psalm 25 which is mainly characterised as a wisdom psalm by scholars on the basis of this feature and because of its proverbial style in verses 12–14. There are alphabetising tendencies also in Psalm 33 without it being an acrostic proper. Psalm 37 is an acrostic psalm and is dominated by didactic exhortations in verses 1–8, most of which involve trusting in God. Clearly the composition of an acrostic is an intellectual exercise and so such psalms are likely to come from a literary milieu. However, whether they are necessarily the product of 'wise' circles is still debatable.

Thus we can find wisdom forms in large measure in a whole range of psalms, but there are only a few psalms in which they are found in large enough quantity for us to classify the whole as a wisdom psalm. It is likely that wisdom has found a place in the liturgical expression of Israelite faith and that its influence is felt widely. The question that remains is whether the wisdom forms that appear are a primary or a secondary influence on the material. It is my contention that, rather than viewing wisdom influence as an editing feature alone, as has been a trend in much recent scholarship, it is likely that it played a role in the formation of psalms at source. Wisdom was a world-view shaping the thought of psalmists as the psalms were compiled, it was part of being educated and able to write and it was not a sphere of life divorced from others. Rather it forms an important place in Israelite liturgical life from early times.

Content

The categorisation of wisdom psalms on the level of content is also problematical because of the difficulty of deciding what kinds of content are typical of wisdom literature itself. E. Gerstenberger also looks for wisdom content in the psalms, what he terms 'outspoken didactic interests and intentions' (1974, p. 219), for example in the introduction to a psalm: 'My mouth shall speak wisdom; the meditation of my heart shall be understanding. I will incline my ear to a proverb; I will solve my riddle to the music of the lyre' (Ps. 49:4); and in 'the topics and motifs of the psalms . . . those also present in other wisdom literature' (p. 219). However, the finding is that often part of a psalm may contain a wisdom motif; for example the same 'teacher's summons' opening as Psalm 49 is found in Psalm 78 which is not generally considered to be a wisdom psalm since most of its concern is with the salvation history of the Israelite people. So the classification is difficult – the presence of any one of the above characteristics is not sufficient to classify a psalm as wisdom. On a more profound thematic level we might want to look for the presence of certain theological elements in psalms such as a concern with retribution (Kuntz, 1974) or with the fear of the Lord (e.g. Psalm 111:10). Crenshaw (1982) argues that the most striking affinities between psalms and wisdom occur in a group of psalms that belong to the genre of 'discussion literature'. He includes in this category Psalms 37, 49 and 73 on grounds of content – they all ask the perennial question about divine justice in the face of the apparent prosperity of the wicked. He also includes Psalm 39 in this category because it twice takes up Qoheleth's motto concerning the vanity of human life (39:5, 11; 39:6). We shall see in what follows how prominent the theme of punishment and reward is in these psalms and how it dominates other concerns.

A basic content that resembles wisdom concerns can easily be found in these psalms. For example, there is an interest in wealth and poverty in Psalm 14, the rich being castigated for their treatment of the poor (vv. 4–6): 'Have they no knowledge, all the evildoers who eat up my people as they eat bread, and do not call upon the Lord?' (v. 4; cf. the parallel in Psalm 53). Psalm 62:8–12 warns against placing trust in riches in true wisdom fashion: 'if riches increase, do not set your heart on them' (v. 10). Wealth however finds its proper place in Psalm 112 which contains a description of the righteous person and his blessings of descendants, wealth and so on. The righteous person is then contrasted with the wicked person who sees the righteous prosper and is angry: 'they gnash their teeth and melt away; the desire of the wicked comes to nothing' (v. 10b). Another common theme of Proverbs is an emphasis on speech, knowledge and words (e.g. Prov. 15:9; 23:9), and we find this in Psalm 19 in the proclamation of the glory of God and in the human response at the end of the psalm: 'Let the words of my mouth and the meditation of my heart be acceptable to you, O Lord, my rock and my redeemer' (v. 14). The second half of Psalm 34 also mentions the power of words when it exhorts, 'Keep your tongue from evil, and your lips from speaking deceit' (v. 13). Another wisdom interest is comparing the wise person and the fool, alongside the righteous and the wicked. Psalm 92, for example, does this in verses 5–8 with reference to the dullard, the stupid and the wicked, who are all contrasted with God's deep thoughts and great works; and with reference to the flourishing of the righteous, as likened to a tree (vv. 12–15). The emphasis on the benefits of a good wife found in Psalm 128:3 recalls Proverbs 31 – 'Your wife will be like a fruitful vine within your house; your children will be like olive shoots around your table' – and the reference to walking in the ways of the Lord in Psalm 128:1–2 recalls the proverbial idea of life as a path.

On a more profound thematic level we may look for the themes that we have seen to characterise Proverbs and that we have used as a yardstick to evaluate the other wisdom books. The first is that of order in the world. A clear link is made with creation in some psalms, for example in Psalms 33:6–9 and 104:1–18 the listing technique used also recalls wisdom genres. Perhaps more striking is the strong emphasis on trusting and hoping in Yahweh found in a number of psalms. Psalm 37 springs to mind with its injunctions to 'Trust in the Lord, and do good; so you will live in the land, and enjoy security' (v. 3). Also, 'Take delight in the Lord (v. 4) . . . Commit your way to the Lord (v. 5) . . . Be still before the Lord (v. 7) . . . Wait patiently for him (vv. 7, 9).'

God is very much at the centre in the wisdom psalms, more overtly so than in Proverbs, and in this characteristic they recall Job and Ecclesiastes. For example, Psalm 32, which mainly consists of thanksgiving, although it also contains a dose of lament (cf. Job), advocates trust in the Lord in verses 10–11: 'Be glad in the Lord and rejoice, O righteous, and shout for joy, all you upright in heart' (v. 11). Because of the centrality of God and the interest in just rewards for the righteous and punishment for the wicked, the ambiguity in events, our second theme, tends to be lost. There is perhaps ambiguity in the fact that some psalms seem to be positive both about God and wisdom and about the possibility of justice in God's dealings with human beings, and yet others portray the rather darker picture with which we are familiar from Job and Ecclesiastes. However, there are no occasions when this is aired as a contradiction; rather, the contradiction exists within the group as a whole, almost by default.

A major emphasis falls on the third theme of punishment and reward which seems to be the most central preoccupation of the wisdom psalms. Psalm 1 contains a contrast between the righteous and the wicked in true wisdom style, although a link is made with the law, which has led some to classify it as a 'torah meditation' psalm (Crenshaw, 1982) rather than putting it in the wisdom category. We may compare Psalm 19, the second part of which is certainly torah meditation, and Psalm 78:5–11 in which there are references to the law in a psalm that is largely one of historical recitation. The contrast between the righteous and the wicked as found in Psalm 1 comes out strongly in the second half of Psalm 34 (e.g. v. 21): 'Evil brings death to the wicked, and those who hate the righteous will be condemned.' In Psalm 36:1–4, 10–12 there is a description of the wicked and an indication that only the righteous have access to the temple (which leads Kselman (1997) to argue that the psalm is an entrance liturgy). In Psalm 37 the psalmist is worried by the prosperity of the wicked (vv. 1, 7b), and the message is that the righteous will come to possess the land eventually, and the wicked will perish. Some psalms question God's system of justice that seems, temporarily at least, to have gone awry, for example, Psalm 49 which concerns the prosperity of the wicked, notably the rich who boast of their riches. The author counters this threat by commenting on the fleeting value of riches, and even of wisdom itself, in the light of death, the great relativiser (v. 10). There is a section on the fate of the wicked and a suggestion that the author will be ransomed from the power of Sheol (v. 15) in the most positive part of the psalm.

Psalm 73 likewise concerns the prosperity of the wicked. It begins with a statement which is shortly to be put to the test: 'Truly God is good to the upright, to those who are pure in heart' (v. 1). It then describes the way in which the author nearly stumbled when he saw the prosperity of the wicked and envied it. There is a glorious description in verses 4–9 of this prosperity: 'For they have no pain;

their bodies are sound and sleek. They are not in trouble as others are; they are not plagued like other people' (vv. 4–5). The turning point in the psalm is in verses 15–17 in which the author realises both that such talk of his envy is false and that the attempt to understand by means of the intellect has failed. His perspective is finally changed on going into the sanctuary where he perceives that the end of the wicked is death and destruction. There are some similarities here with the book of Job which too bewails the prosperity of the wicked, and in which Job is answered by a theophany in which God does not respond to his questions on a strictly intellectual level. Rather, it is the experience of God that leads him to repentance. So the author of Psalm 73 realises that riches are fleeting and that God is to be cherished more than any earthly desires. The final section of the psalm is confident of God's continuous presence and the author feels remorseful of previous attitudes. This is a profound psalm and, as von Rad writes, 'in the description of the gravity of the attack and above all in the expression of absolute security in God, this poem far surpasses the point of view of Pss. 37 and 49' ([1970] 1972, pp. 205–6). Psalm 94 contrasts the pit, dug for the wicked, with God's treatment of the righteous (vv. 12–15). References to fools in verse 8 and comparison of the thoughts of man to a breath in verse 11 are wisdom elements in this psalm which is mainly to be classified as a lament.

   The fourth major theme of life as the supreme good is featured here, but mainly in the stream of lament or protest against this belief, recalling Job or Ecclesiastes. We might think of Psalm 39 which characterises human life as vanity. In Psalm 39 there are also references to the wicked and to guarding one's way, reminiscent of Proverbs, which gives the whole a didactic character. Psalm 49, in antithesis of the idea of life as the supreme good, has a strong preoccupation with death, with some similarities with Ecclesiastes, and some likeness to the speeches of Job in the mention of Sheol and the Pit. Also, Psalm 90, a lament on the transitory nature of human life, has similarities to themes in Ecclesiastes in particular, and verses 5–6 compare this frailty to that of plants as in Job 14:5–12. Von Rad ([1970] 1972) classified Psalm 90 as a wisdom psalm on the grounds of its gloomy pessimism, and, although few would agree on this genre classification, the mood is in line with the other psalms mentioned here. This fourth theme therefore mainly seems to appear in its antithesis – life may have been good once, but this presupposition is now under serious threat in the light of the suffering of the righteous and the frailty and uncertainty of human life.

The fifth theme was that of confidence in wisdom which can be found in this material, despite the questioning that also appears. Psalm 51:6 states: 'You desire truth in the inward being; therefore teach me wisdom in my secret heart.' Psalm 25 likewise exhorts, 'Make me to know your ways, O Lord; teach me your paths' (vv. 4–5), and there is an emphasis on the benefits of instruction in verses 8–10, 12. There are thus strong exhortations to pursue the way of wisdom, and confidence in the quest is undermined only by the laments and questioning that we also find in this genre of material. There is no material on the final theme of the personification of wisdom.

The wisdom psalms then are an interesting microcosm of a number of the themes that we have found so far. In their diversity they span the whole range of wisdom thought from maxim-making to severe questioning of the principles of justice. The theme of punishment and reward is revealed as a major focus of wisdom psalms and does suggest some link with the 'discussion literature', and yet, many of the forms of wisdom found in the psalms are traditional ones, mainly paralleled in Proverbs, and we find the basic content of proverbial wisdom in some psalms. Mainstream wisdom is thus represented, even though the major thematic thrust is starting to show the influence of a more questioning spirit.

Context

Wisdom was thought by older scholars, and is thought by many recent ones, to be more of a late literary influence than an early cultic one. Interesting suggestions have been made for a wisdom shaping of the Psalter (see Whybray, 1996), focusing in particular on the beginnings and endings of 'books' of psalms and of the whole Psalter (e.g. Brueggemann, 1991). On the question of context, it is usually held that those psalms that display wisdom influence are generally to be regarded as non-cultic. Mowinckel (1955) argued that the wisdom psalms are essentially prayers and, although addressed to human beings, they are first and foremost addressed to God. He saw wisdom psalms therefore as non-cultic prayers which nevertheless were influenced by the styles and ideas of cultic psalms with which sages were constantly coming into contact. According to him, these wisdom psalms were included in collections of cultic psalms at a later date. Recent work has begun to question this view. It is argued by Whybray (1996), for example, that such non-cultic compositions may well have been used for the purposes of worship, and that there may well have been a closer connection between religious observance and instruction than is often maintained. He cites evidence from Daniel 6:10–11 and from the author of Psalm 119, who prayed to God seven times a day, to argue that psalms of all types might well have been used in the context of prayer. Psalm 1, too, speaks of the individual in the language of wisdom as one who meditates on Torah. We need therefore to bear in mind that wisdom may well have found a place in meditation, in prayers and in religious observance generally. This would certainly be true of later wisdom, as in the use of prayers in Ben Sira and the Wisdom of Solomon, but we need to consider the possibility of its being true earlier in the development of wisdom too.

Cross-fertilisation with wisdom thought may be a late development – Mowinckel assigned a late date to these psalms on grounds of style. He argued that the 'learned psalmography' 'tries on the whole to keep to the old paths and adhere to the old rules of composition' (1955, p. 213) without doing so strictly, which leads to a disintegration of the style. He saw sages as 'the learned and inspired collectors of the holy traditions of the ancients' (1955, p. 210). Others have seen wisdom psalms as evidence of a later branching out of the activities of the wise, as noticed with regard to an interest in prophecy in Ben Sira and the Wisdom of Solomon. L. G. Perdue (1977) and others have even seen a closer link between wisdom and cult, in the post-exilic period. But why this preoccupation with 'later'? Is it not possible that there was a closer link from the beginning between wisdom and cult and that these psalms and others were the product of early groups of psalmists influenced by the wisdom tradition? Could it not suggest that wisdom was part of the self-understanding of the people, and thus it found expression in their cultic life just as all other areas of their life and history did? The Psalter represents the great variety of traditions in Israel – it would be odd if wisdom were not represented. Of course, it may be that interest in apparent injustice developed after the exile and that the 'discussion psalms' of 37, 49 and 73 fit better at that time. But the influence of wisdom on many other psalms shows it was not a phenomenon to be pushed into a theological ghetto.

I suggest that there was a link with the cult from early times – an interest in order, in God's creative role and in the human order that derived from the divine. Many of the psalms under discussion are found to have a cultic context apart from the wisdom sections. It seems reasonable to suggest that the didactic elements of these psalms may well have found a cultic context. E. Gerstenberger (1991) suggests a post-exilic cultic context when discussing Psalm 37. He writes, 'didactic psalms, rather were composed for and were used in early Jewish worship services, very probably on the local level, outside Jerusalem' (1991, p. 159).

I suggest too that the interest that wisdom has in creation and order may lead us to include some cultic psalms concerning those issues in our 'wisdom' corpus; Psalm 104 for example, which also employs listing techniques. In fact we might look for evidence of that tension between a cosmology that sees God as creator and an anthropology that concerns human need for God, which we have found to be a key theological thread running through the wisdom literature. Whether we call such psalms 'wisdom psalms' or even consider them products of wisdom influence, is however another matter.

So after consideration of these psalms we find that, whilst some such as 1, 34, 37, 39, 49 and 73 have a good claim to be called wisdom psalms, we have been more inclined to speak of wisdom's having an influence on the Psalter as a whole. Such a range of psalms and the number of criteria for including them in the category of wisdom make it difficult to determine their contribution to the definition of what constitutes wisdom. It does seem to be largely on the basis of affinities with other wisdom literature that psalms or parts of psalms are included and so we cannot add to the definition from this starting point. Furthermore, it is difficult to know where to draw the line when undertaking this classification. There seems sufficient evidence to suggest that Israel's sages eventually participated in, or directly influenced, the cultic life which finds expression in the Psalter but it is hard to know the full extent of this influence. Whether it was a primary influence on the formation of ideas or whether it was a later literary shaping of psalmic material by the wisdom writers is a question that remains open, although I have tried to argue for both possibilities.

6:   WISDOM'S INFLUENCE IN THE OLD TESTAMENT

By the strength of my hand I have done it, and by my wisdom, for I have understanding. (Isa. 10:13a)

Questions of definition become most relevant when we look at the rest of the Old Testament to find wisdom influence. The danger is that we will find wisdom around every corner and hence devalue the concept itself. And yet we have seen that there are different levels of wisdom influence. Whilst little of the rest of the Old Testament would normally be designated 'wisdom literature' – and we shall go on to evaluate that claim in relation to certain narrative texts – we can find the influence of wisdom in its pages and it is this that we shall look at first in relation to the prophets (see Lindblom, 1955). The question that comes to the forefront here is the same as the one we faced with the wisdom psalms: whether wisdom is a primary influence in the formation of material, or whether it tends to be the product of later editing, in scribal circles responsible for putting together or supplementing books in their final form. I suggest that the latter approach has been emphasised too much, and that, instead, wisdom is to be seen as a primary influence, not just the product of educational circles, but also part of the fabric of knowledge as experience that shapes the thought of prophet and priest in ancient Israel. Rather than there having been separate groups of priests, prophets and sages, so different from each other that they were unaware of each others' world-views, we shall see how in fact wisdom brings these groups closer together from earliest times, in its formative influence on material.

The influence of wisdom on other material makes it clear that there was an alternative mode of revelation through the everyday, through human experience of the world and of God, that was able to inform all areas of Israelite life and complement other world-views. The wisdom view, while it does not encompass the historical, can nevertheless be found in more historical presentations of the faith, and so its exclusivity works one way and not the other.

Other areas of Israelite life did not permeate wisdom until the later apocryphal wisdom material emerged; however, wisdom ideas did influence other areas of life, albeit in subtle and sometimes small ways. We have seen this at work in the wisdom psalms, so now let us turn to the prophets in which we will look for the influence of wisdom forms, content and contexts. This is well-trodden ground and there will be an opportunity here only to indicate the nature of the debate in each case.

Wisdom influence in the Old Testament prophets

Amos

It was argued thoroughly by H. W. Wolff ([1964] 1973; [1975] 1977) that the eighth-century prophet Amos was closely associated stylistically and theologically with the wisdom tradition. The prophet was clearly well versed, was acquainted with the geography, history and social customs of nations outside Israel and was aware of standards of ethical behaviour common to all peoples. If wisdom is to be seen as a basic education then this is certainly true here. The oracles to the nations in the first part of the book, for example, make use of wisdom forms, notably that of graded numerical sayings 'For three transgressions . . . or for four . . .' (1:3, 9, 11, 13; 2:1, 4, 6). It has also been argued that they draw on a wider ethical code than any Israelite one (Barton, 1980), and Amos makes ethical behaviour the prerequisite of divine favour along wisdom lines. So maybe Amos got some of his ideas from wisdom circles. If wisdom was a more widespread phenomenon than just groups of wise men and schools of wisdom for the educated, this influence is hardly surprising. So Wolff finds the background of the prophet's preaching in early wisdom. Building on the work of E. Gerstenberger (1962), who traces the relationship of traditional proverbial wisdom to many rhetorical forms found in the prophets, Wolff points to stylistic usages such as rhetorical questions (e.g. Amos 3:3–6), woe oracles (e.g. Amos 5:18), exhortation (e.g. Amos 5:14–15), numerical heightening (e.g. Amos 1:3f.), antithetic expressions (e.g. Amos 5:4–6), reiteration and so on to support his thesis as well as drawing on arguments from wisdom vocabulary. Vocabulary parallels are found in particular in the concern for social justice (Amos 2:6–7; 4:1; 5:11–12; 8:4, 6). From the point of view of content he discerns a lack of concern about idolatry, an interest in astronomy, an attack on luxurious living, a moralistic conception of salvation, and so on. From all this he concludes that Amos was steeped in the wisdom tradition. It may well be that those finding wisdom as the only key to unlock the thought of Amos are being one-sided – others have found an interest in the cult to be an equally important idea in his thought. However, there is clearly a strong influence in his thought here, to be taken alongside other influences in the shaping of this, in many ways, most fresh of prophecies. Amos was adept at imitating and borrowing forms from other spheres of life and using them in a fresh context in Amos 1:3— 2:6; 3:9–11; 4:4, 6–12; 5:1–3, 18–20; 9:7–8a (Dell, 1995). He has used the wisdom tradition at points to illustrate or intensify his message in language that would have been familiar to his hearers, e.g. riddles, comparisons and popular proverbs. However, there is no sense in which he is to be seen as a member of a group of the wise or as part of an intellectual élite of society in that he is described in Amos 1:1 as 'a herdsman and dresser of sycamore trees' (Amos 7:14b) and even if he was a sophisticated tradesman, this kind of model does not easily fit his situation.

Wolff's view has been challenged by J. L. Crenshaw. Crenshaw points out that since wisdom is based on experience, a degree of similarity in terms of style, vocabulary and theology between wisdom and prophetic and priestly traditions is unavoidable. While Crenshaw agrees that Amos employed sapiential terminology and that he owed terms and themes to the cult, he has a different emphasis that he wants to place. He writes: 'The language, ritual, and theology of the theophanic tradition pervade the book of Amos' (1968, p. 213). His argument is that Amos on numerous occasions reversed cultic theophanic language when he put his prophecies into words. Theophany is the advent of the deity in order to proclaim his word, and Crenshaw also extends the meaning to include God's interference in nature and history. He argues that Amos, in his use of words, is actualising Yahweh's activity which up until this point was expressed in a repeated, symbolic way in the cult. Crenshaw's ideas have stimulated interest once again in cultic possibilities whilst retaining a wisdom element, and he has made an interesting link-up between the two areas that resembles our discussion in relation to wisdom psalms. However, this view has been criticised on the grounds that we cannot in fact be certain of a festival context in which theophany was a central focus.

Hosea

In the context of the question about what kind of prophet Hosea was, the influence of ideas about nature on his thought is often pointed out (e.g. Hos. 8:7; 5:12; 6:4b; 7:11). E. Sellin ([1910] 1923) suggested that Hosea's interest in images of nature and animals meant that he may have been a farmer and cattle-breeder, rather like Amos, before he was called. Like Amos he is subject to an amalgam of influences and his precise social history is unknown. His role was chiefly to warn Israel of the coming judgement and to criticise the corrupt cult. Yet from time to time he used images and forms from everyday life, in the manner of proverbial wisdom (e.g. Hos. 4:11; 14:9; 10:7), as a means of conveying Yahweh's message. A. A. Macintosh has recently stressed that wisdom traditions are an important formative influence upon Hosea – they are 'but one element woven into the texture of his prophecy' (1995, p. 132). Examples of wisdom forms are a call in 5:1 that resembles a teacher's summons, numerical heightening in 6:2, similes (Hos. 6:4; 7:4; 7:11; 7:16; 10:7) and admonitions (Hos. 10:12). Other allusions include a possible reference to proverbial teaching about boundaries in Hosea 5:10, use of wisdom-type vocabulary such as 'to know' (see below) and 'to understand' (Hos. 4:14), and contrasts between good and evil (Hos. 14:3). H. W. Wolff did a similar study of wisdom in Hosea ([1961] 1974) to his Amos study and also included among his list of wisdom forms the proverb of Hosea 8:7 and the prophet's perception of the workings of nature in Hosea 2:23–4. The final verse in Hosea 14:9 is clearly from wisdom circles, and many have regarded it as a later addition, perhaps from redactional 'wisdom' editors: 'Those who are wise understand these things; those who are discerning know them. For the ways of the Lord are right, and the upright walk in them, but transgressors stumble in them.' However, it can be seen as part of the wisdom context that Hosea is using and transmitting to his hearers, in that it picks up catchwords that are used in the prophecy (e.g. 'stumble' in Hos. 4:5; 5:5; 9:2 and 'transgress' in Hos. 7:13 and 8:1), and it uses the antithetical style of wisdom. G. Fohrer went as far as to posit that, because there are so many wisdom elements, 'Hosea was educated at a wisdom school which served primarily for the training of royal officials' ([1965] 1970, p. 393). While few scholars would probably agree, and many would limit the wisdom influence to an acquaintance with popular sayings that had a wider parlance rather than with a formal education, at least it demonstrates the extent of the influence.

It is interesting that, in the context of his so-called covenant theology, Hosea uses images from the natural world. Fohrer writes:

> Hosea is unfamiliar with any covenant theology. The few occasions when the word 'covenant' appears do not refer to any relationship between Yahweh and Israel... To describe the relationship between Yahweh and Israel, Hosea, like the young Jeremiah after him, uses instead images and metaphors drawn from family life and from the world of plants and animals. ([1965] 1970, p. 424).

There are three covenant references, the first in Hosea 2:18 to a new and ideal covenant framed in natural terms, 'I will make for you a covenant on that day with the wild animals, the birds of the air, and the creeping things of the ground'; the second in Hosea 6:7 in which there is a historical retrospect, 'At Adam they transgressed the covenant'; and in Hosea 8:1b a reference to Israel's 'having broken my covenant and transgressed my law'. So in fact we have three very different formulations of covenant in Hosea. The first of these looks as if it might have connections with the wisdom emphasis on order and creation in that Hosea 2:18 clearly has overtones of the covenant with Noah in Genesis 9 – a bond between God and creation which can never be broken. This also links up with the wisdom idea of the world order being composed of right relationships between God and humanity, between God and nature, and between human beings and the natural world (see Dell, 1994a). This is likely to be an idea found in the cult – one finds these links in psalms such as Psalm 104. It may therefore suggest an ideal, non-legalistic, perception of covenant as relationship that either preceded or existed alongside the more usual formulations of covenant with which we are familiar in the Old Testament (see Murray, 1992). It is interesting that Hosea formulates this idea in 2:18 when speaking of a future for Israel – a new covenant that will replace anything that went before. Maybe he is here thinking of a past concept of covenant that was lost and needed to be revisited.

Let us look at this suggestion in connection with the key phrase 'knowledge of God' that appears a number of times in Hosea. This may contain a legal element. This is undoubtedly the case since no society can function without law, and the reference in Hosea 8:2 aligns covenant and law. In 4:6 Hosea accuses the priest of having 'forgotten the law of your God', and this is set in the context of the destruction of the people by lack of knowledge. However, how far is this a particular set of laws or a wider moral law or a set of ethical rules? D. F. Morgan suggests that 'knowledge of God' for Hosea was not simply cultic instruction, but the phrase was used to cover all aspects of individual morality. In the context of a discussion of wisdom influence on Hosea, he writes: 'While it may be unwarranted to consider Hosea's concern with knowledge as wisdom influence, nevertheless this may be an example of an interface between wisdom, prophecy and cult which ultimately led to the equation of cultic torah with wisdom' (1981, p. 73). I find this an interesting suggestion, that Hosea may well be drawing on a wider ethic with links with wisdom's emphasis on the importance of knowledge. It may be that later interpreters found more legalistic overtones in Hosea's words than were in fact originally the case, and that a broader ethic was later brought into line with an explicit legal code. If this is the case then Hosea would have been largely appealing to common sense and experience, an important teaching model that would have reached an audience in a profound way. Part of the 'knowledge of God' that has been forgotten by the people is the action of God in history, itself the ground of the relationship between God and the people. This history would have been recited in the cult and provided a profound reason for Hosea's chastisement of a society which seemed to have forgotten the significance of such deeds.

Micah

Micah was clearly an educated person and as such may well demonstrate wisdom influence in his thought. However, there is little evidence apart from a few wisdom forms and images that may be no more than common parlance – such as the woe oracle (Micah 2), the lamentation using nature comparisons (1:8f), the concern with good and evil in 3:2, the interest in bribery in 3:12, and the use of wisdom vocabulary in 4:12 and 6:9 (see Wolff, [1978] 1981). It would be difficult to differentiate Micah from those whose cause he champions on the basis of these wisdom traces which were probably commonplace.

We might ask on a more profound level, where does Micah get his ethics from? Is he reviving an idea of the covenant that had fallen into disuse, or is he basically propounding a new way at looking at the relationship between Yahweh and Israel, one based on justice and righteousness, instead of on election and mistaken covenant loyalties? There is no mention of a covenant in his work, nor even the idea found in Amos that the people should have known better because they were elected (Amos 3:2). Of course, the people may have known of Amos' arguments or Isaiah's pleas, but here the argument from covenant loyalty is not used. The impression is of a new declaration, a fresh way of looking upon the relationship between Yahweh and the people. The people's response to Micah is documented. They say, 'Do not preach . . . one should not preach of such things' (2:16). They appear to be shocked by what he has to say. Their view of God is different: 'they lean upon the Lord and say, "Is not the Lord in the midst of us? No evil shall come upon us" ' (3:11). The question is raised: is Micah therefore drawing on a wisdom-type ethic from a broader sphere than the covenantal one?

A second question is, what is Micah's picture of God? He seems to be a God of power, described using images from nature in chapter 1 and in terms of Yahweh's use of foreign rulers to implement his purposes in chapters 1—3. He is also a God to whom nature bears witness in chapters 1 and 6, a feature that links up with the universal overtone of chapter 1. Maybe Micah's God is bigger than his contemporaries have been trying to make him – he is certainly more powerful than they would like to think. The universalism in the first chapter, for example, could be part of a wider influence upon Micah from the wisdom tradition with its international flavour and non-particularistic stance. This can be seen in conjunction with the references to nature as Yahweh's witness in Micah 1:2–4 and 6:1–2.

Isaiah

Isaiah was also an educated person and some have advanced the theory that he was a professional wise man at court (Whedbee, 1971) or that he had been a member of 'the wise' before becoming a prophet (Fichtner, [1949] 1976) which would explain his criticisms of them (Isa. 3:1–3; 5:21; 30:1–5; 31:1–3). There are clear examples of wisdom forms in his thought, including an opening teacher's formula, 'Hear, O heavens, and listen, O earth; for the Lord has spoken' (Isa. 1:2), as well as use of woe-forms (e.g. Isa. 5:8, 11), wisdom vocabulary (e.g. 'to know', 'to understand' and 'counsel'), proverbial passages (e.g. Isa. 2:22; 3:10–11), and comparisons with the animal world (e.g. Isa. 1:3). Whedbee argues that Isaiah is rich in proverbial as well as parabolic speech and that wisdom is a major feature of his style. In Isaiah 1:3, 5:7 and Isaiah 28:23–9, for example, Isaiah uses parables, and 28:29 is a summary appraisal which states: 'This also comes from the Lord of hosts, whose counsel is wonderful, whose wisdom is great.' Further, in Isaiah 10:15 and 29:16 the prophet uses wisdom methods of argumentation. However, while wisdom forms are found in his work, we should not be too hasty in drawing inferences about his social position from this, since wisdom was most likely a more widespread commodity than just the preserve of the royal court. He uses the wisdom tradition to criticise the status quo in his attempt to bring people back to Yahweh.

Where does he get these ideas from? The thought of other eighth-century prophets can be shown to be the product of a variety of influences from the thought-worlds of cult, law and wisdom, and this is equally the case in reference to Isaiah. He may well have taken his lead from earlier prophets such as Elijah on the involvement of Yahweh in political affairs, and his social preaching may owe something to Amos or other contemporaries. And yet his message is sufficiently distinctive for that not to be the whole picture. There are a few hints of Israel's legal traditions in Isaiah; for example the duties of judges towards the poor are listed as in the book of the covenant in Exodus 20:23—23:19, thought to predate Isaiah, and yet his ethical ideal seems to go further than that. J. Jensen (1973) has suggested that when Isaiah uses the word 'torah' he means 'wise instruction'. J. Barton (1979) has interestingly argued for a basis in 'natural law' for Isaiah's social condemnations which may link up with the wider ethic of the wisdom tradition. Further, Isaiah, like the other eighth-century prophets, does not seem to have a developed view of covenant on which he is drawing. This raises the question: where has this notion of divine order come from?

There is generally thought to be a good case for seeing Isaiah as influenced by the wisdom tradition in the Old Testament, although we find a certain amount of scholarly disagreement as to how that mainly manifests itself (see the discussion in Williamson, 1995). If we leave aside the question whether an influence by wisdom was a mark of an educated person, there is on a basic and profound level an understanding of order that Isaiah has in common with wisdom. He speaks of God's wisdom (5:19–24) which he contrasts with 'you who are wise in your own eyes' (v. 21). He appeals to common experience rather than special revelation. Rather than relying on humans and their alliances, Isaiah tells his contemporaries to trust in Yahweh. Although we might think at first that this sounds rather anti-wisdom, since much wisdom originates from human activity and experience, when we consider the more theological side of the wisdom coin we start to see a link. When we think of the figure of wisdom, for example, in Proverbs 8, she is the path to life, to order, to justice – the means of God's revelation of all these things to human beings. It may even be that this picture was itself influenced by Isaiah. Although many of the proverbs do not explicitly mention Yahweh, there is a presupposition of a divine order at the limits of human knowledge that humans will never fully comprehend by means of their own understanding. Full knowledge will be mediated by God through wisdom. The idea of a divine plan at work is also found in Proverbs: 'The human mind plans the way, but the Lord directs the steps' (Prov. 16:9). Further, the whole proverbial scheme of two paths – one leading to life and the other to death; one leading to wisdom, the other to folly; one leading to fulfilment, the other to despair – seems at home in Isaiah's thought.

The concerns that Isaiah has with drunkenness, pride and arrogance are all at home in the wisdom literature: e.g. Proverbs 20:1; 21:1; 31:1–8; 13:10. Isaiah's attack in 5:21 on those who are 'wise in their own eyes' is a direct quote from Proverbs 3:7. Even Isaiah's criticism of cultic sacrifice is found in Proverbs 21:3 in a comparative sense: 'To do righteousness and justice is more acceptable to the Lord than sacrifice.' It was H. H. Schmid (1966) who argued that Isaiah's ideas on order had much in common with the Egyptian concept of Ma'at which is often likened to the divine principle of Wisdom as found in Proverbs. He saw justice and righteousness in Isaiah's thought as the two foundations of that order, which he found in other ancient Near Eastern cultures to be a 'cosmic order'. We may link this up with the emphasis on nature in Isaiah. Schmid makes the point that nature works according to a system of order as God intended it, whereas human beings work against such an order (e.g. Isa. 28:27–9). There are hints of a more universal view of God in Isaiah too which would suggest a perception of him as creator rather than solely as redeemer. I do not wish to draw the conclusion from these observations that Isaiah was not a prophet but was a wise man (see Whedbee, 1971). But what it does show is that prophets were heirs to different traditions and that there was a separate tradition from covenant and history in existence on which Isaiah could draw. I therefore see all the eighth-century prophets as in different degrees influenced by such a tradition, and I wish to emphasise its existence alongside and maybe even prior to some of the more historical and legal traditions that we so readily associate with Israelite faith.

Jeremiah

Like the eighth-century prophets, the seventh-century prophet Jeremiah shows that he is influenced by the forms of wisdom such as the rhetorical question (Jer. 2:14; 8:4–5; 18:14; 23:28); numerical formula (Jer. 15:3); a wisdom poem (Jer. 17:5–11); and the proverb, although the latter is very much adapted to his message (e.g. Jer. 13:12–14; 15:12; 23:28; 31:29). There is a preoccupation with understanding – or lack of it on the part of those he is addressing (Jer. 4:22; 8:7; 9:23–4) – an interest in Yahweh as creator (Jer. 10:12f; 31:35f.), a concern with retribution (Jer. 12:1f; 17:11) and social justice (Jer. 50:20–9). In Jeremiah 10:23–5 we read: 'I know, O Lord, that the way of human beings is not in their control, that mortals as they walk cannot direct their steps' (cf. Prov. 20:24). There are also contrasts drawn in wisdom style between those who are wise, who heed God's message, and those who are foolish, who lack understanding of God's will; e.g. Jeremiah 17:5–11 begins with a traditional wisdom contrast between those who trust in mere human beings and those who trust in the Lord. It speaks of God testing the mind and searching the heart and ends with a proverbial saying which compares the partridge on borrowed eggs with the person who amasses wealth unjustly (cf. Isa. 3:10–11, 26:7–10).

There is an element of polemic in Jeremiah that J. Fichtner ([1949] 1976) also finds in Isaiah, against a group of 'the wise' who claimed to possess counsel and who were statesmen in the service of the kings of Judah. There also seem to have been 'wise' people who interpreted the law. Jeremiah raged against those who claimed a false wisdom that ran counter to the demands of Yahweh (see McKane, 1965). There is a question whether the references to 'the wise' in Jeremiah illuminate our understanding of the context of wisdom. It does suggest different groups of educated 'wise' people in the court, some with a political function, others with a more scribal role. Are they to be seen as a class (Jer. 18:18), or is this simply a generic term for those offering counsel against whom Jeremiah found himself opposed? There is a particular concern with 'the wise' in Jeremiah 4—10 (8:8–9; 9:23–4), including those of foreign nations (10:7). R. N. Whybray (1974) makes the point that the expression 'the wise' in Jeremiah's thought does not seem to be a technical term; rather all the 'wise' are united by the fact that they do not perceive what Yahweh is doing. Jeremiah, in his attack on the wise, employs a clever technique: he uses a certain amount of the language and presuppositions of the wisdom tradition to mount the attack and to bring people back to a truer faith in Yahweh.

Ezekiel

Like other prophets, Ezekiel uses proverbs (Ezek. 12:22; 15:2; 16:44; 18:2). Two of these quotations of proverbs are set in the wider context of allegories, themselves sometimes a wisdom form; the other two are in the context of a disputation, using a proverb to set peoples' views straight. Ezekiel 18:3 quotes a proverb in order to say that it is wrong. Ezekiel also, like Isaiah and Jeremiah, attacks the kind of wisdom that leads people to think that they are self-sufficient and need not listen to Yahweh. He makes reference in this context also to foreigners, e.g. in chapter 28 on the inhabitants of Tyre. Interestingly, in Ezekiel 'counsel' is ascribed to the elders rather than the wise (Ezek. 7:26) in whose guidance the people are no longer to put their trust. Once again, as with Isaiah and Jeremiah, the prophet Ezekiel employs the forms and images of wisdom, attacks the wrong kind of wisdom and tries to set people upon the right path again in tune with the will of Yahweh.

We may also connect these wisdom links to an interest in creation. The vision of the dry bones seems to me to be the most vivid picture of an overturning of the natural order that can be effected by Yahweh. It is part of the demonstration of his power. The restored land is also an image presented in idealistic natural terms. Thus it is not only history that will repeat itself in terms of a new Exodus, but the natural order itself will witness to the restoration of the nation to her land.

Deutero-Isaiah

We also find in Deutero-Isaiah some use of wisdom forms: proverbial forms (Isa. 49:24; 55:8, 13); woe oracles using nature imagery (Isa. 45:9); and rhetorical questions concerning God as creator in the context of a prophetic disputation (Isa. 40:12–14). There is a reference in Isaiah 44:25–6 to the way the wisdom of the wise looks foolish in the light of the wisdom of God. Wisdom is not generally seen as a major feature of his work on the level of form; however, there are some important thematic links, especially in the concern for God as creator. The wisdom literature takes its starting point from the revelation of God in nature and in human relationships. Unless we see wisdom as an entirely late phenomenon in

Israelite thought, we cannot ignore that its stress on God as creator of all may not have been part of earlier tradition. There may not have been an emphasis in wisdom on salvation for all – this element may be new here – but there is the sense that all people are part of God's concern, and that moral norms of righteous and wicked behaviour are the most decisive ones when it comes to relationship with God.

It is often noted that in Deutero-Isaiah creation and redemption are closely linked. Is this a new development? It seems to be within prophecy, and yet the link was already made in the liturgy in psalms such as Psalm 104. As part of the emphasis on creation we find reference to a new creation – nature is to be restored to an ideal state in which the wolf will lie down with the lamb. At the second Exodus, the natural order will be overturned. This language is perhaps metaphorical to express the wonder of the new act of God, and yet it is interesting that this terminology is used. Is Deutero-Isaiah picking up here on an alternative covenant tradition such as we noted in Hosea 2? If not a covenant, it may well be an older creation tradition, perhaps linking up with the wisdom tradition, that is being reiterated here in idealistic terms.

Wisdom in the Pentateuch and historical books

There are sections of the Deuteronomistic History, notably the Succession Narrative in 2 Samuel 9—20 and 1 Kings 1—2, as well as sections of the Pentateuch, in particular the J document in Genesis 1—11 and the Joseph story (Gen. 37—50), that have been considered the productions of wisdom, notably of the Solomonic enlightenment. In more general terms, work has been done on the use of traditional sayings in the historical books and on wisdom influence in Deuteronomy. C. R. Fontaine (1982) argues that the use of proverbs in new contexts demonstrates a vital tradition operating at all levels of society. This idea undercuts that of wisdom as the preserve of an educated class, and suggests, once again, that the genre was more widespread. She studies Judges 8:2; 8:21; 1 Samuel 16:7; 24:13 and 1 Kings 20:11 in the light of wisdom and of folklore studies. She concludes in favour of a tribal wisdom that employed wisdom forms as part of a shared world-view. Daily wisdom in the form of observations drawn from experience is the focus of her study. This is a refreshing change from those who wish to stress the highly literary nature of wisdom, which, whilst it has its place, is clearly not the whole picture. We shall see that the evidence from the Pentateuchal and narrative texts seems to point in the same direction that the prophetic material did, that is in the direction of an early wisdom influence on material subsequently written into new and more historical contexts. Rather than wisdom concerns having shaped the interests of the authors and later editors of texts, the influences appear to be more primary than this.

Deuteronomy

An emphasis on natural law can be found in the book of Deuteronomy complementing the more nationalistic codes of law that it contains. It is often remarked about Deuteronomy that it contains a wider ethic than the strictly law-based injunctions that one would expect in a law book. For example, the laws about slaves (e.g. Deuteronomy 23:15, 'Slaves who have escaped to you from their owners shall not be given back to them', which corresponds to Proverbs 30:10, 'Do not slander a servant to a master') go beyond legal stipulations to provide a prescription of a more humane nature, characteristic of wisdom and rather oddly placed in a legal code.

M. Weinfeld (1972) studies the links between Deuteronomy and the concept of wisdom, finding use of a conventional sapiential idiom, 'too wonderful', in Deuteronomy 30:11-14, echoing Job 42:3, Psalm 139:6 and Proverbs 30:15-33, but expressing the view that, unlike wisdom which is remote and inaccessible, this teaching is accessible. An emphasis that may well be sapiential in Deuteronomy is that of easy comprehension by all. The phrases 'word of God' and 'the fear of the Lord' are both paralleled in Proverbs and Deuteronomy. Their origins in wisdom literature get across a sense of the universal. Other phrases, such as the term 'abomination to Yahweh' as a condemnation of wrongdoing, are found only in Deuteronomy and the book of Proverbs, and are paralleled in Sumerian and Egyptian wisdom literature in reference to other gods. The section in Deuteronomy 27:15-26 abounds in affinities to wisdom literature in its listing of offences such as dishonouring parents and

the unjust treatment of aliens, and so on. Often, more general proverbs are reformulated as laws in Deuteronomy, e.g. Proverbs 20:10
and Deuteronomy 25:13–16 on the issue of false weights. There are
laws in Deuteronomy that have no parallels in other law codes but
do have parallels in wisdom literature; e.g. injunctions about removal
of boundaries and falsification of weights have verbal parallels in
Proverbs 22:28 and 23:10; and Proverbs 11:1 and 20:10, 23. There is
a stress on humanism that pervades Proverbs and Deuteronomy;
there is also an exhortatory and didactic tone in Deuteronomy that
resembles the exhortations of father to son in the book of Proverbs.
The idea that life is good and that just reward will be forthcoming
and will lead to happiness is found in both, as is a universal attitude
to possession of land. In Deuteronomy these ideas take on a more
nationalistic tone, and often covenantal language is used. Thus
observance of the commandments equals wisdom and understanding
(Deut. 4:6), and it is the people of Israel who observe the laws and
commandments who are 'a wise and discerning people' in greater
degree than others. This air of the more universal takes its starting
point from the wisdom tradition.

The contextual question whether Deuteronomy was specifically composed by scribes rather than by priests, possibly Levites,
has been discussed by Weinfeld (1972) on the basis of similarities
noted with the wisdom literature. He argues that there was a literary
renaissance at the time of Hezekiah, reference to which can be found
in Proverbs 25:1, where 'the men of Hezekiah' have a role, and that
Jeremiah 8:8 suggests that wise men were connected with the law:
'How can you say, "We are wise, and the law of the Lord is with us",
when, in fact, the false pen of the scribes has made it into a lie?' This
theory about Hezekiah resembles the Solomonic enlightenment
theory but places a broadening out of wisdom influence at a rather
later period. In fact Weinfeld also places the Succession Narrative
(see below) in this period, seeing it as scribal editing rather than the
product of an earlier wisdom renaissance. If we leave aside this
question of a later context, which may nonetheless have some
mileage, it is interesting to note the influence of wisdom upon Deuteronomy in much the same way that we have done with the
prophets. Weinfeld sees the Israelite conception of wisdom as having

changed in this period of the seventh century and, while it is important to see wisdom as a developing and changing phenomenon, his thesis rests too much on theories about context. It is possible, in my view, that wisdom, as part of the general thought-world of the time, had an influence on new formulations of material without necessarily being the product of particular groups of scribes.

Pentateuchal texts

The criteria for including material in the wisdom category start to become diverse in relation to Pentateuchal texts. The emphasis in the Yahwist on the human condition, notably in Genesis 2—3 (Dubarle, 1946; Alonso-Schokel, 1975), an interest in creation, a concern with order and human responsibility in Genesis 4—11 (Brueggemann, 1972) and a parallel to the story of the fall in the Babel material in Genesis 11 (Whybray, 1974), may add up to indicate wisdom influence in the realm of ideas. It is difficult to know whether the association of ideas here happened in the oral stages of transmission of material or whether we see here the work of a literary genius, the J author, someone possibly educated in a wisdom school.

The inclusion of material from Genesis 1—11 raises a broader question of the relationship between wisdom and creation theology; a tradition is revealed with an interest in God as creator and the response of humans to his call. This has also been raised in relation to the prophets where an alternative tradition seems to be present that takes its starting point from God's activity in creation and nature and the response of human beings to that action. Rather like the figure of wisdom in Proverbs 8, who represents God's creative work and calls to humans to be part of the natural order, we see Amos, Hosea, Isaiah and Jeremiah drawing on ideas of order in society that is being threatened by human pride and over-confidence. The creation and Babel stories contain this parable too – a message about human pride. Far from being a glorification of human achievement these stories suggest a severe criticism of a world-view that puts too much emphasis on the human and not enough on God. The wisdom tradition calls for this balance in the relationship, one that is offered freely by God and misused so readily by humankind.

Other contenders for wisdom influence in the Pentateuch

but outside the Genesis material are the birth narrative of Moses in Exodus 1:8—2:10, which B. S. Childs (1965) classifies as a historicised wisdom tale, and the Song of Moses in Deuteronomy 32 which opens with a wisdom exhortation (Boston, 1968). Both may well have been formulated in wisdom terms long before being placed in their present contexts.

G. von Rad in 'The Joseph Narrative and Ancient Wisdom' ([1953] 1966c) was the first to note the strong emphasis on human achievement in the Joseph narrative, accompanied by a 'delight in all things foreign' (p. 293, 1984 edn), with an Israelite rising to great power in Egyptian circles as an administrator and right-hand man of Pharaoh. Joseph is described as possessing ideals of the wisdom writers – patience, prudence, the fear of the Lord. He is the successful administrator, with knowledge of when to be outspoken and when to offer good counsel, and he exercises self-control in his relationships. The question is raised: is this a deliberate portrayal of Joseph in idealistic wisdom terms, or is it part of the tradition of the story of Joseph that already saw him in this light? There is some debate whether this narrative is simply to be regarded as a product influenced by wisdom, or whether it should actually be seen as wisdom literature, in having the forms, content and context of wisdom in large measure. It stands apart from the material around it and so can be regarded as an independent piece, a wisdom novella perhaps. Furthermore, the strong emphasis on human achievement in the narrative, with Joseph as a paradigm of the ideal administrator, suggests a possible context in the court. However, one has to espouse a view of the context of wisdom that has a courtly setting at the centre in order to view this as wisdom literature, and some scholars (Coats, 1973) have had serious reservations about its inclusion in this category. Also the strong emphasis on human achievement and the hiddenness of God's purposes in the narrative make it unlike the more overt presentation of divine purpose in Proverbs. Further, it is a weakness in von Rad's thesis that a number of the parallels that he uses are from Egyptian wisdom, notably from the Instruction of Amenemope, rather than Proverbs.

The Deuteronomistic history

A similar question as was raised by Weinfeld (1972) in reference to Deuteronomy pertains to Solomon in 1 Kings 3—11: is his
wisdom being highlighted in a time of increased interest in courtly
wisdom, as R. B. Y. Scott (1955) suggests in the time of Hezekiah, or
is this emphasis the product of Solomon's own time? It would be odd
if the major section regarding wisdom's 'hero' Solomon was not
influenced by its genres. It seems unlikely that the portrayal would
be all retrospective, since Solomon must have got his reputation for
wisdom from somewhere, and yet, as with other heroes of Israel's
past, some glorification of their person is feasible. It is likely that this
narrative was cherished in wisdom circles over a considerable period
of time.

The other contender for this early Solomonic period is the
Succession Narrative in 2 Samuel 9—20 and 1 Kings 1—2, another
easily distinguishable section of text of a high literary quality that
may well have had a separate origin and that appears in particular
to praise human ingenuity. The connection between the Succession
Narrative and wisdom was first made by von Rad in 1944 and taken
up by Whybray in 1968 in a monograph in which he argued that the
Succession Narrative was an attempt to teach the doctrines of
the wisdom schools in a dramatised form. He pointed out similarities
with the Egyptian literary tradition as well as the Israelite narrative
tradition, arguing for particular parallels with the Instruction of
Amenemhet and the Story of Sinuhe, as well as possible links with
Egyptian royal novel genre. He likened the Succession Narrative to
the autobiographical narrative form found in Israelite wisdom and
also noted wisdom forms such as the simile and comparison. On the
level of content, he found themes of wisdom of folly, an emphasis on
counsel, retribution and on Yahweh as in ultimate control. He writes:

> There seem to be good grounds for concluding that on many fun-
> damental matters – the importance attached to human wisdom and
> counsel both in public and private affairs; the acknowledgement of
> their limitations and of the unseen, all-embracing purpose of God
> and of his retributive justice; the relatively small attention paid to
> the cult; and the stress on the importance of ethical conduct,

humility and private prayer – the Succession Narrative agrees closely with the scribal wisdom literature as represented by Proverbs rather than with the sacral tradition of Israel. (Whybray, 1968, p. 71).

He posited a context in the monarchic period, seeing this narrative as another product of the Solomonic enlightenment, a combination of propagandist political novel and wisdom instruction.

Summarising comments on the Pentateuch and historical books

In this Pentateuchal and historical material we can see the clear influence of the wisdom tradition – some forms and content are there. The question of their inclusion under the wisdom umbrella revolves around the issue of context. If the wise were a group based at the court, responsible for teaching on the one hand and administration on the other, it is possible that they might have produced 'court narratives' such as the above. If the date of this activity was at the time of Solomon the conclusion that this material is wisdom literature of a formative type is feasible. However, given the uncertainties surrounding the positing of this kind of context and the possibilities of the production of such material at a later date – the time of Hezekiah perhaps – it might be safer to speak of wisdom influence on this material rather than trying to pin it down as wisdom literature. It takes our definition of wisdom literature into a more didactic and courtly context than much of the discussion has allowed up until now and it pushes the balance between anthropocentric and theocentric decisively in the anthropocentric direction. Although wisdom is, in large part, about human capability, this aspect should not, in my view, be overstressed.

Daniel, mantic wisdom and apocalyptic

Another character with possible wisdom links is Daniel, who has been judged a model wise man along similar lines to the figure of Joseph. Again, we are in the realm of the court and may wish to see Daniel as the 'wise' courtier (cf. Ezek. 28:3). Daniel 1:3–5 describes the young Israelite men of the court, summoned by the

Babylonian King Nebuchadnezzar who had besieged Jerusalem. They are described as being 'versed in every branch of wisdom, endowed with knowledge and insight, and competent to serve in the king's palace'. Among them is Daniel, who soon becomes the interpreter of dreams in the manner of a rather different kind of wise man, as found in Babylonian culture and throughout the ancient Near East, well versed, it seems, in the science of omens, divination, the interpretation of dreams and of the future. This branch of wisdom has come to be known as 'mantic wisdom' and closely matches the activities of Babylonian scribes, whom Daniel is concerned to put in their place. J. Goldingay (1989) writes of the different perception of wisdom in Daniel in his commentary: ' "Wisdom" ... denotes in Daniel the supernatural intuition of an interpreter of dreams or omens, that wisdom which also belongs supremely to God (2:20) and which as his gift makes Daniel outstanding among sages (1:17; 2:21, 23).' It is interesting that the nature of wisdom as divine revelation is more prominent here than the human and practical side of wisdom, although the young men of the court were no doubt educated in this aspect too.

Two questions are raised by a consideration of the book of Daniel; the first is about the possible inclusion of the book as wisdom literature, a categorisation that is not widely supported. Rather than include the book, even chapters 1—6 only, as wisdom literature, to speak just of wisdom influence is widely agreed by scholars to be preferable here. Wisdom influence on Daniel is operating on two levels, first on the primary level of the content of the story and the character of Daniel, and second on the level of the author who may well have himself been a scribe, possibly one of the Hasidim (Da. 12:1–4). However, the consensus of opinion is that Daniel is apocalyptic rather than wisdom in genre, apocalyptic itself possibly being seen as a scribal phenomenon (Smith, 1975). Rather along the lines of other books of the Old Testament, the book of Daniel is influenced by wisdom both in its earlier and later stages of composition, rather than being generically a wisdom book.

The second question raised by a discussion of Daniel is that of the relationship between wisdom and apocalyptic. Prophecy was traditionally seen by scholars as the forerunner of apocalyptic, although this was countered famously by von Rad who saw it as having its roots in wisdom. He highlighted knowledge as 'the nerve-centre of apocalyptic literature' ([1958–61] 1962b, p. 306) and spoke of the determinism of both later wisdom and apocalyptic that was lacking from prophecy. Von Rad saw the principal influences from wisdom to be the sciences of dream interpretation and the understanding of oracles and signs, that is, mantic wisdom. This kind of wisdom has its starting point in revelation rather than in human experience. Thus it is not mainstream wisdom of the kind that has been under discussion so far, but a fresh development in wisdom that most closely parallels apocalyptic. Apocalyptic, like wisdom, is concerned with the acquisition of knowledge; however, it is usually concerned with knowledge for a chosen few rather than for all. Apocalyptic may well have grown out of a synthesis of prophecy and wisdom that begins to emerge in a wider intellectual milieu. Yet, the genre tends to arise as a result of a particular historical crisis, as in Daniel, and it limits wisdom to a few chosen ones, such as Daniel himself who alone has God's divine wisdom at his disposal (unlike the earlier wisdom tradition in which it is available for all). Thus apocalyptic may well have grown out of wisdom as well as out of prophecy, but it is a later variety of wisdom that has itself developed beyond the mainstream wisdom literature of the Old Testament. I shall go on to mention this again in Chapter 11 in connection with Qumran.

7: WISDOM'S ROOTS IN THE ANCIENT NEAR EASTERN WORLD

The wise man is girded with a loin-cloth. The fool is clad in a scarlet cloak. (Sumerian proverbs: Assyrian collection iii: 13–14 (K8206), Lambert (1960), p. 232)

When attempting to define the limits as well as the context of ancient Near Eastern wisdom we find ourselves in a similar quagmire to that already experienced in reference to wisdom psalms and to wisdom influence within the Old Testament. Once again, as with the psalms, texts are generally ranged alongside Israelite ones on the basis of similarities in genre and concern. It is interesting that the Instructions from Egypt have been classified as wisdom literature only on the basis of the parallels with Israel. When we examine the material from the cultures of the ancient Near East, we find that Proverbs appears to have most in common with Egyptian wisdom and some Semitic wisdom, such as the Wisdom of Ahikar, and we find that Job and Ecclesiastes tend to have more in common with Mesopotamian genres. We have seen how scholars of the past have been quick to extrapolate contextual conclusions as to the origin and nature of Israelite wisdom on the basis of these extra-biblical parallels. It is interesting to note that in the ancient Near East the scribal class are not an entirely separate group. The distinctive character of wisdom literature is a result of the requirements of the genre rather than a reflection of the group from which it derived. Another point to make is that millennia divide these texts from their Israelite counterparts. The question is raised whether developments that took place in more advanced cultures many centuries before Israel emerged as a monarchic state can really be seen as close parallels given the time lapse. However, on the other side of the argument, we have evidence from archaeological finds that texts were copied over and over again by scribes as part of the learning exercise and so were transmitted from one culture to another by this method, having been familiar over a long period of time.

There is little doubt however that the origin of the wisdom enterprise is to be found in the ancient Near Eastern world rather than in Israel herself. Similar kinds of texts to Proverbs, Job and Ecclesiastes appear in the civilisations of Egypt and Mesopotamia millennia before they appear in Israel. The phenomenon of wisdom – the basic pattern of making observations about the world and family relationships – is common to most cultures in the world. However, it is interesting that there was no formal wisdom tradition in the countries surrounding Israel (Weeks, 1994). In the ancient Near East, wisdom was not praised as a great prize, it was not a separate genre of material, and seldom was there a moral content to it. By contrast, all these characteristics would be true of the Israelite wisdom material. Scholars of Egyptian and Mesopotamian 'wisdom' thus only range texts together on the basis of what is known of the character of Israelite wisdom. W. G. Lambert writes in his book *Babylonian Wisdom Literature* that ' "Wisdom" is strictly a misnomer as applied to Babylonian literature ... Though this term is thus foreign to ancient Mesopotamia, it has been used for a group of texts which correspond in subject-matter with the Hebrew wisdom books' (1960, p. 1). This suggests that we are not going to get much further in our definition of wisdom by the use of these parallels since they are themselves defined as wisdom on this comparative basis. It also shows that we may be wrong in separating the wisdom enterprise into a separate category as scholars have been prone to do in biblical studies. Just as wisdom texts were part of a wider enterprise in the ancient Near East, so they were in Israel too.

Ancient Sumerian wisdom

The most ancient wisdom activity comes from ancient Sumer, the first of the Mesopotamian civilisations. The Sumerians developed a system of writing and this, plus many of their myths, was formulated by the second half of the third millennium BC and was eventually taken over by the Babylonians by 1000 BC. We know that there was a large scribal fraternity, and excavations at Nippur have revealed what is thought to be a scribal quarter of an old Sumerian centre. We know from tablets dating from the second millennium BC that teachers and pupils, trained in the *edubba* (tablet house), were the educated people of society. Sumerian tablets containing a description of school life give us an insight into this. In it the daily school routine is described thus:

> I recited my tablet, ate my lunch, prepared my [new] tablet, wrote it, finished it; then they assigned me my oral work, and in the afternoon they assigned me my written work. When the school was dismissed, I went home, entered the house and found my father sitting there. I told my father of my written work; then recited my tablet to him, and my father was delighted. (Kramer, 1958, pp. 42–3)

We also have a satire on school life from ancient Sumer in which a father chastises his son for wasting his time in pleasures instead of applying himself to study. Those designated for high office in palace or temple were trained in these schools which were found in the major centres of Sumerian civilisation. There was also an archival function attached to the *edubba* – especially when the culture was under threat, the need was felt to write down important stories, myths or history.

Interestingly, we find Sumerian proverbs which reflect an agricultural background and concern with family life that resemble the Proverbs, particularly Proverbs 10:1—22:16 (Gordon, 1959). These may well have been oral at an early stage, but were used as part of the school curriculum later on. They appear on numerous tablets mixed in both subject matter and type in that short sayings are mixed with fables, anecdotes, and so on. Some tablets contain the material in two languages, Sumerian and Akkadian, and it is striking that later copying of earlier material is often found with the same formations and groupings of material. Many of the tablets are damaged, and the proverbs can be very obscure and difficult to translate. The 'Assyrian collection' is a dialogue between an Amorite and his wife who change roles, and clothes and woo each other. This is interspersed with proverbial sayings such as rhetorical questions, 'Seeing you have done evil to your friend, what will you do to your enemy?' (ii 35–7), straightforward proverbs, such as 'A people without a king is like sheep without a shepherd' (iv 14–15), and religious admonitions, such as 'It is not wealth that is your support. It is (your) many of his ideas owe their origins to Hellenism. Sirach 14:18, for example, has been likened to Homer's *The Iliad* 6, lines 146–49. The *Poems of Theognis* (book 1) also contains practical advice similar to the wisdom literature. The question is raised: was there a deliberate attempt by Ben Sira to use 'Gentile' parallels and thus demonstrate the worth of such literature, or are these links simply reflecting the fact that such ideas were around at the time? Furthermore, did Ben Sira simply borrow Greek material when he could fit it into his Jewish world-view, or was his interest more extensive than that? Hellenism has been seen by some as the major influence in his teachings (e.g. Middendorp, 1973) and others have pointed to a link with Stoic philosophy (Winston, 1989). Middendorp argued that Ben Sira sought to build a bridge between Greek culture and Jewish tradition in his extensive use of Greek sources, while V. Kieweler (1992), in opposition to Middendorp, argued for a diversity within both Judaism and Hellenism that meant that Greek thought was already part of Jewish tradition. He argues that, rather than being a bridge between Judaism and Hellenism, Ben Sira is within a Judaism forced to confront the phenomenon of Hellenism. Both authors acknowledge some Greek influence here, although there is a question about Ben Sira's motives for inclusion of such ideas. A. Di Lella argues that Ben Sira's appropriation of Hellenism is conservative, 'characterized by a tendency to preserve or keep unchanged the truths and answers of the past because only those are adequate as solutions for present problems' (1966, p. 139). He argues that Ben Sira had, on his travels, encountered the effects of Hellenisation, possibly meeting Jews whose faith was challenged by it. His book would thus have been written to bolster the faith and confidence of these Jews rather than to provide a polemic against Hellenism (which is a common suggestion). There is a good deal of quotation of or allusion to scripture: e.g. Deuteronomy 6:5 in Sirach 7:29–30; Job 19:21 in Sirach 13:23; Isaiah 51:3 in Sirach 15:6; and the greatest dependence is on Proverbs, e.g. Proverbs 8:22, Sirach 1:4; Proverbs 8:18–19, Sirach 1:16–17, and so on. This suggests that the author was certainly at home in Jewish tradition, although there are indications that he was well versed in both Egyptian and Greek literature too.

god' (ii 42–3; see Lambert, 1960, pp. 220–33). Although many of the genres of ancient Sumer were taken over by the emergent Babylonian culture, that of proverbial sayings is almost entirely lacking. They already had the Sumerian collections and some Akkadian texts, a product of Semitic culture that existed alongside the Sumerian, and it may be assumed from letters and works of literature from Babylonian circles that proverbs at least circulated orally. Thus their absence is surprising. One further Sumerian wisdom text that is sometimes likened to Job is 'Man and his God', a lament as a result of sickness and misfortune. There is the strict idea that a person's misfortune is a result of sins committed – in fact, no person is without sin, having been born sinful – and so it is the human who is always to blame, never the gods. However, the answer suggested by the author of this particular lament is that the only thing to do, despite the apparent injustice, is to keep praying to the gods and, in fact, the piece ends happily with the deliverance of the sufferer. There are similarities with the overall pattern of Job in that a case study is used and the poem moves from lament to restoration, although there is little that resembles the radical questioning of God's motives that we find in Job.

Babylonian wisdom

There is a marked difference between the Sumerian outlook and that of the Babylonian, the crux of which can be described as the move from the gods to human beings. Lambert describes the change thus:

> So long as the gods were simple personifications of parts or aspects of nature a wonderful reality pervaded thought. But as soon as human reason tries to impose a man-made purpose on the universe, intellectual problems arise. We can see the beginning of this change in the Sumerian, Man and his God, although there is not a radical questioning of the all-powerful nature or other motives of the gods. The big problem in Babylonian thought was that of justice. If the great gods in council controlled the universe, and if they ruled it in justice, why? (1960, p. 10).

Here we start to find literature paralleling Job, such as the Babylonian dialogue between a man and his god in which the man says 'The crime which I did I know not' (line 13, published by Nougayrol, 1952). There was also a developing preoccupation with death, resembling that of Ecclesiastes; the Epic of Gilgamesh, for example, originally a Sumerian myth, is rewritten in a Babylonian version in which the hero is tormented by the idea of dying and wishes to achieve immortality. Scribal families seem to have continued, with links to the temple and we find as time goes on less reference to an *edubba*, suggesting that learning and religion became closely linked.

To the Cassite period of Babylonian culture (1500–1200 BC) belong some of the main products of Babylonian literature to be likened to Israel's wisdom literature, notably Ludlul bel nemeqi – I will praise the Lord of Wisdom – and the Babylonian Theodicy, both of which treat the problem of the failure of the 'piety as a guarantee of prosperity' principle. Ludlul asks why his god Marduk allows his servant to suffer both at the hands of others and from various diseases. The sufferer was a man of authority and a model of piety, forsaken by the gods and despised by others, from the king to his slaves. He is afflicted with disease which has emanated from the gods, and he asks why he has met the fate of a wrongdoer when in fact he was a model of piety. There then follow three dreams which indicate the appeasement of Marduk's wrath, followed by restoration, being freed from his disease. There are clear parallels here with the book of Job.

The Theodicy contains an orthodox friend who maintains the traditional view that piety leads to prosperity against the view of the sufferer, very much in the manner of Job's friends. The problem of why humans oppress each other is raised and the idea that a personal god can provide protection is rejected. Bypassing the original presupposition of a just universe set up by the gods, the sufferer and his friend agree that the gods made humans prone to injustice. No answers are given, although the friend has recourse to the idea of human limitation in the understanding of sin, and the remoteness of the gods who alone can reveal a person's sin. There is also a note of resignation in the suggestion by the sufferer that he might give up all social responsibilities and live the life of a vagrant, for which he is chided by his friend, who appeals to the sacredness of the institutions he proposes to abandon. This futility is continued in the Dialogue of Pessimism which declares all life to be futile (resembling Ecclesiastes), but goes a step further and decides that suicide is the only good. Lambert has recently argued that the Dialogue of Pessimism is rooted in older thought and was known in Mesopotamia before 1600 BC. This suggests that Ecclesiastes was presenting an older theme from the thought-world of the ancient Near East for the ears of an Israelite audience. In the Counsels of a Pessimist, the pessimism is countered by an urging of people not to neglect farm, family or gods. This work contains practical advice, resembling Proverbs, including material on the importance of proper speech and a humanitarian concern for the poor, although there is a section on religious duties.

Semitic parallels

I mentioned a parallel ancient Semitic culture above, as evidenced in Akkadian texts, and have discussed Babylonian works. J. Day (1995) has recently drawn attention afresh to the importance of further Semitic parallels to Israel's wisdom literature. The 'wisdom of the people of the east' is mentioned in 1 Kings 4:30 and there is probably a direct acknowledgement of the wisdom of Massa in north-west Arabia in Proverbs 30:1 and 31:1. There is also the connection of Job with Edom, and Day points out that the whole tenor of Job in its engagement with the problem of theodicy is more Semitic than Egyptian. Semitic influence could well have shaped later Mesopotamian texts such as Ludlul bel nemeqi and Day notes that an Akkadian work comparable to this has been found at Ugarit (RS 25.460 in *Ugaritica* V, Paris, 1968, pp. 264–73). This suggests that the righteous sufferer theme was known early on in Canaan, thus suggesting local influence on Job rather than just influence from more distant cultures. In a discussion of Ugaritic texts, L. Mack-Fisher makes the interesting observation that Babylonian wisdom forms a more important background than Egyptian: 'Egypt was not unimportant for eastern Mediterranean didactic literature, but at Ugarit the Babylonians were their teachers' (1990, p. 76). She points to the interest in nature wisdom in Ugaritic texts and the importance of the Epic of Gilgamesh, an old Babylonian edition of which treats the futility of human endeavour and which we have seen to be comparable to Qoheleth.

An often-forgotten parallel to Proverbs is the Wisdom of Ahikar, lines 81–2 of which form a close parallel to Proverbs 23:13–14 (see Greenfield, 1995). It is an Aramaic composition dating possibly to the seventh century BC and so is an interesting contemporary document to the biblical proverbial material. The contrast between the righteous and the wicked found in Proverbs is present here as is the graded numerical saying and interest in animal proverbs. The admonition to 'my son' is found in Ahikar rather than in the Egyptian Instructions and there is a possible personification of wisdom in Ahikar, if 'it' is taken as 'she', which resembles that in Proverbs 8: 'Even to gods is it precious, to it for ever belongs the kingdom, in heaven it is treasured up, for the lord of holiness has exalted it' (Ahikar vii 95, Cowley's translation, 1923).

Egyptian wisdom

I have begun this survey of the ancient Near Eastern material in ancient Sumer, Mesopotamia and among other Semitic parallels rather than beginning among the Egyptian material, in part to redress the extensive attention given to the Egyptian context in the quest for parallels to Israelite wisdom (Bryce, 1979; Heaton, 1994). When we turn to the Egyptian material we immediately find some similarities of sentiment to Ecclesiastes. In 'A Dispute over Suicide', an Egyptian didactic text from the end of the third millennium BC, we find a man weary of life and of his own soul and contemplating suicide. However, on the realisation that he may not be given a decent burial, his soul decides that a life of pleasure is preferable and it becomes a debate between the man and his soul. In the end they decide to stay together whatever the outcome.

However, the major parallels to Israelite wisdom from Egypt are the Instruction texts which compile wise sayings with the aim of instructing a young man as to how to lead a successful life and develop the kinds of qualities admired by others. One of the oldest instructions is that of the Vizier Ptah-hotep (2500 BC) to his son and successor. The Instruction opens with a description of old age that resembles the poem in Ecclesiastes 12, although it is more explicit in its reference:

> The heart sleeps wearily every day. The eyes are weak, the ears are deaf, the strength is disappearing because of weariness of heart, and the mouth is silent and cannot speak. The heart is forgetful and cannot recall yesterday. The bone suffers old age. Good is become evil. All taste is gone. (Instruction of Ptah-hotep 10; see Pritchard, 1969, p. 412)

We might also draw attention to a similar description of old age found in Sumerian proverbs: '[I was] a youth [but now] . . . my black mountain has produced white gypsum . . . my teeth which used to chew strong things can no more chew strong things . . .' (lines 27–32; see Alster, 1974, p. 93). This latter description is arguably a closer parallel than the Egyptian example because of the more metaphorical language. The Instruction of Ptah-hotep continues with advice on a whole range of subjects including relationships with wife and friends, avoidance of avarice and licentious behaviour, correct behaviour at table and an emphasis on discipline and self-control – all well-known themes from the proverbial literature of Israel. There is also a religious element in the idea of divine sovereignty: 'He whom god loves is a hearkener, [but] he whom god hates cannot hear' (line 545, Pritchard, 1969, p. 414).

There are numerous instructions from different periods in Egyptian culture, containing a plethora of maxims and advice on all kinds of subjects. We know that the Instruction of King Amen-em-het (2000 BC) was copied over and over again and became an important text for schoolboys. It was in fact a piece of political pro-paganda written to support the succession to the throne of Sesostris I (1971–1928 BC) after the assassination of his father King Amen-em-het. The dead king warns his son to trust no one and to beware of helping others who might just get the better of him. As in ancient Sumer, this material was used for teaching purposes in scribal schools attached to the principal state institutions. Interestingly, an Egyptian student is rebuked in one text: 'I am told that you have given up books, and are reeling in pleasures . . . If only you knew that wine is taboo' (R. J. Williams, 1972, p. 218). We might compare this to a Sumerian text that expresses the same idea: 'Night and day, you waste in pleasures. You have accumulated much wealth, have expanded far and wide, have become fat, big, broad, powerful and puffed' (Kramer, 1967, p. 245). We have the Instruction of Ani from the period of the New Kingdom (1540–1070 BC) which is the work of a temple scribe writing for his son, and the background appears to be more domestic and middle-class. There is an emphasis on the importance of silence, on the friends made, on the avoidance of strange women and strong drink and so on. There is a strong urging to grasp the opportunities of a scribal education and a strong religious element.

The Instruction of Amen-em-opet (or Amenemope) (before 1000 BC) is a thirty-line Instruction, often thought to be in a different league from other Instructions. It has been particularly studied by biblical scholars because of the parallels with Proverbs 22:17—24:22 (especially Proverbs 22:20 in the reference to 'thirty sayings'). By rearranging the order of the admonitions the two texts can be seen to contain very similar sentiments, notably in the section 22:17—23:11, and scholars continue to disagree over the question of borrowing, in particular the question whether the entire instruction is paralleled in the whole section of Proverbs from 22:17—24:22 (see the discussion in Whybray, 1994b). These parallels, if not demonstrating borrowing on the part of the Israelite writer, certainly reflect cultural interchange. For example, there are maxims on many subjects such as false weights, land boundaries, dealings with angry people, proper attitudes towards money, envy, greed and so on. There is an air of acceptance about this work that suggests that the writer believes that everything has been determined in advance: 'Man knows not what the morrow is like ... One thing are the words which men say, Another is that which the god does' (lines 13, 16–17; see Pritchard 1969, p. 423). God is the source of morality and this is the ground for behaving in a moral manner. In Amenemope two types of behaviour are contrasted – that of the silent man and that of the rash or heated man. This corresponds to the contrast in Proverbs between the righteous man and the fool, although it is interesting that the categories are rather different. There are proverbs on the merits of silence and the inappropriateness of rash talk but not in the section

Proverbs 22:17—24:22. There is however no acknowledgement of Amenemope of the sort that one finds in Proverbs 30:1 of Agur and 31:1 of Lemuel, king of Massa, and some scholars have recently expressed caution in stating too direct a dependence between the two works (see Whybray, 1994b).

The Instruction of Onchsheshonqy (400 BC) is an anthology of sayings that indicate a rural background in which school work had to be done in conjunction with farm work. There are 550 sayings covering all aspects of behaviour including an emphasis on the right words, caution in making friends and trusting people, and in relations with women. There is the same emphasis on God as the ordainer of all things and as the principle of justice. Some of the sayings are rather roughly formulated and rather obscure. It is interesting that these different Instructions betray different contexts which suggests that the quest for a court context as the primary one has been overstated.

Other Egyptian works include Kemyt, a manual giving conventions for letter writing, the Instruction of Khety, son of Dauf, otherwise known as 'The Satire on the Trades', which includes the satirising of manual workers and elevating the role of the scribe above all others. These were both copied over and over again for up to a thousand years in the same manner as the Instruction of Amen-em-het. Another such text was the 'Hymn to the Nile' celebrating the river Nile in psalmic style. Other texts were more narrative in style such as the 'Story of Sinuhe', an autobiographical narrative recounting the adventures of a high-ranking palace official who fled on the assassination of his king and settled in Palestine, rising to high position (see also the 'Story of Wenamun'). There are some parallels here with the Joseph story in Genesis. Another often-copied text is a piece of political propaganda written in support of King Amenemet I, called 'The Prophecy of Neferti' which contains a prediction with hindsight of a new and just king. 'The Satirical Letter of the Scribe Hori' is a satire about the pompous and pretentious scribe with a sarcastic questioning of a pupil on the geography of the region, full of rhetorical questions in similar manner to God's questions from the whirlwind in the biblical book of Job. We also find in Egypt songs that have been likened to the Song of Songs in which invariably a woman speaks or is praised. Although there is also a clear parallel here between Egyptian love poetry and the Song of Songs, this is arguably outside wisdom genres.

From Egypt, then, the main forms of 'wisdom' literature that we find are the Instruction, the Royal Testament, the lament; the work of political propaganda, and possibly the love song. The most striking absence from all except later Egyptian texts is the sentence form which is so primary in Proverbs. The parallels between Egyptian Instructions, manuals for worldly success, and similar forms in Proverbs 1—9 have long been noted (Kayatz (1966) argues that the balance of probabilities is in favour of Egyptian influence on Proverbs 1—9). There is also the striking parallel between the Instruction of Amenemope and Proverbs 22:17—24:22. A close relationship can also be found between the Egyptian concept of Ma'at, an order in which practical concerns and divine order meet, and the figure of Wisdom in Proverbs (Ma'at is also described in 'The Tale of the Eloquent Peasant', 310–315, although there are no speeches here such as Wisdom gives). We also find the Royal Testament form in Egyptian literature (e.g. the Instruction of Merikare and the Instruction of Amen-em-het), in which a Pharaoh records his advice to his son and heir. This is often thought to form part of the background to Ecclesiastes 1:12f, the Solomonic fiction.

We also find some more pessimistic texts that bewail the decadence of society and its moral decay, although it is social injustice rather than a questioning of divine justice that is of concern. The problem of theodicy does not seem to have been a major preoccupation in Egypt. Some more political productions come from the Middle Kingdom period, such as the Instruction of Merikare and the Instruction of Amen-em-het. We may also consider the 'Hymn to Aten' and its relationship to Psalm 104. The hymn celebrates creation in similar manner to the psalm, although with more emphasis on human development and racial variety than the Israelite psalm:

> How manifold it is, what thou hast made! They are hidden from the face [of man]. O sole god, like whom there is no other! Thou didst create the world according to thy desire, Whilst thou wert alone: All men, cattle and wild beasts, Whatever is on earth, going

upon [its] feet, And what is on high, flying with its wings. (Pritchard, 1969, p. 370).

Assessment of these findings

One cannot therefore deny that Israelite wisdom is part of a broader ancient Near Eastern phenomenon. This raises the question: was there direct borrowing and a strong formative influence on Israelite wisdom, or are these parallels simply likely developments within cultures with similar world-views? The extent of borrowing is difficult to evaluate, but certainly cultural interchange is likely. While some of the parallels have perhaps been overstressed and wisdom too readily seen as the 'foreign element' in Old Testament thought in the light of such links, it is hard to deny the influence of a wider thought-world on the development of Israelite wisdom. In fact much Old Testament thought can be related to ancient Near Eastern concepts and myths – wisdom is not a special case. We can perhaps argue that the genre of wisdom forms an important bridge between the ancient Near Eastern world and the religion of Israel. But it also retains its own distinctive Israelite character as it developed according to the needs of a particular people – Israel borrowed, but she also created.

At some point in time, the influence of the wisdom of foreign nations infiltrated into Israel; it is often thought to be during the period of Solomon when trade and connections with abroad seem to have been strong. However, one might argue for the possibility of a fairly sophisticated court structure already under David, a legacy from Canaanite patterns. Furthermore, whilst the court of Solomon seems a likely contender in Israel for such activity, we should not forget the 'men of Hezekiah' (Prov. 25:1) and other possible later court contexts. There may alternatively have been a slower in-filtration of wisdom ideas into the early thought of Israel than simply cultural interchange at a court level – an influence from the Canaanite world around them, a natural human tendency towards the search for experiential knowledge, and a basic, cultic tendency towards nature and creation which led indirectly to wisdom influence in the form of experiential knowledge and ethical norms. A more sophisticated and literary tradition however also emerged, one that was the preserve of a more literate class, and it is this tradition that may have flourished in either court, temple or school in an Israelite context. Thus, while the roots of the proverbial tradition may well have been oral and less formal, the actual writing down of the proverbial sayings is likely to have been a more scholarly exercise. It was those with education and a position at the court who had the time for leisure, for learning and for writing.

It is on the question of context that interest in ancient Near Eastern parallels has focused. We can find similar forms and content to Israelite wisdom in Egyptian and Mesopotamian parallels, but is it right to extrapolate the context of one to the other? It is clear that there was no one role for wisdom in any of these nations. Thus while the king and court remain at the centre of the enterprise, we know that in ancient Sumer *edubba* or tablet houses abounded in major cities. Egyptian wisdom, in its use of the instruction form, was clearly primarily used for teaching purposes for the training of a large administrative class centred on the court. There are, in addition, texts that suggest that a predictive role was also important. However, in ancient Sumer the educational role appears to be only one of the functions; another important one is archival, and, although the issue of kingship is at the centre of concern, there is interest in the natural world (e.g. animal and plant fables; cf. 1 Kings 14:9), there is a link with the temple and concern with the proper worship of the gods. Among Akkadian works, the king is at the centre of the wisdom exercise, but also the professions are described as springing from a similar capacity to be wise. Wisdom is not simply an intellectual matter, since in fact only three literate kings are attested in Mesopotamian history; rather, reverence for the gods was perceived as the mainspring of wisdom. Mesopotamian wisdom also had a cultic and magic aspect.

The quest for parallels is a difficult issue and caution against overusing parallels is timely. In recent years, there has been more caution among scholars in drawing such sociological parallels. S. Weeks (1994), for example, has questioned whether Egyptian models of education really provided such a convincing background to Israelite wisdom, and even E. W. Heaton (1994) has backtracked on some of his more far-reaching claims about Egyptian parallels. Yet no culture exists in a vacuum and the parallels suggest that there is cultural interdependence. Egyptian parallels have been the most looked at, so may we not suggest with L. Mack-Fisher (1990) that due attention should also be paid to Mesopotamian influence? It is clear that the strongest parallels are in the more religious lament texts. In the area of context, the Mesopotamian background indicates a broader range of possibilities for wisdom activity which might fit better in the Israelite context, where to force the material only into a court and administrative setting has been exposed as one-sided. The idea of a tablet house in Israelite cities has not been attested by archaeological evidence, but would seem a plausible model (Lemaire, 1981). This would fit also the broader oral context of proverbial sayings as well as the production of the literature itself being a more educated concern. It is also clear from Mesopotamian parallels that both palace and temple were important centres for training bureaucrats, and that many versed in wisdom went into cultic service. The diversity of context therefore that seems to characterise Mesopotamian wisdom – as well as its diversity of form that gives us the parallels to Job and Ecclesiastes – might suggest a more workable model than the Egyptian one.

We have seen in this chapter how the ancient Near East provides us with knowledge of the origins of the wisdom enterprise, its forms and content, and with a number of contexts in which wisdom was practised. We need to evaluate how far we can extrapolate from this context to the Israelite one, and we may wish to reflect on how far this advances our definition of Israelite wisdom – it certainly has a contribution to make to questions of the origins of forms and ideas, and reveals interesting educational contexts in which wisdom was practised. It has underlined the international nature of the wisdom, and yet the differences with Israelite wisdom have underlined the distinctiveness of the enterprise in Israel itself.

8: ECCLESIASTICUS/BEN SIRA

Whoever holds to the law will obtain wisdom. (Sir. 15:1b).

Ecclesiasticus or the Wisdom of Jesus, Ben Sira (abbreviated to Ben Sira in what follows) is often said to have first made the link between Wisdom and Torah, the Law, and this is certainly true in reference to Wisdom personified, whose teaching now embodies the Torah. However, we have seen that a close relationship exists between wisdom and law in Deuteronomy and in a few contenders for the wisdom psalms category, for example Psalms 1, 19, 78; and so maybe it would be wrong to deny all contact between the genres before this point. Yet, after the Exile, we can more readily speak of a broader intellectual tradition in which the borders between groups such as prophets, priests and wise men are becoming more blurred (Whybray, 1974). It is probably a natural step for Ben Sira in the second century BC to equate following the paths of wisdom with following the Torah. G. von Rad remarked that it was rather ironic that wisdom started on the sidelines of Israelite tradition but, once equated with the Torah, it became central in Israelite thought. He wrote:

> At a later date, not precisely ascertainable, there was a decided movement into the realm of theology. Wisdom teaching became the custodian of centralities of the faith and approached man's environment with the whole import of the quest for salvation – it asked about the meaning of Creation . . . Indeed, in odd inversion of its origin, it increasingly became the form par excellence in which all Israel's later theological thought moved. ([1958–61] 1962a, pp. 449–50)

Role

Jesus Ben Sira gives us an insight into his own awareness of his role as a wisdom teacher (Roth, 1980). In Sirach 38:24 we read: 'The wisdom of the scribe depends on the opportunity of leisure; only the one who has little business can become wise.' He then goes on to list the various trades, very much in the manner of the Egyptian The Satire on the Trades. He speaks of the role of the wise man in relation to the law and the prophets, indicating a broad role for the wise of his time and a possible link with the temple. In Sirach 39:4 we read of his role of counselling the powerful and travelling widely, even at risk to himself. And in Sirach 51:23–30 it is clear that Ben Sira is in the business of training young men in a school context (Harrington, 1980). Yet despite these strong indicators that Ben Sira stands in the wisdom tradition as it changes and develops, he has also been seen as a priest (Stadelmann, 1980) with strong prophetic aspects to his identity. It is clear that we must not presuppose that Ben Sira's belongs to the wisdom category without first assessing its forms, content and context in the manner that we have done with the other major wisdom books. After the next section we will go on to ask two questions. First, is it wisdom literature? And second, what are the distinctive concerns of this book?

Structure, date and setting

First, however, an outline of the structure of the book and consideration of date and setting is appropriate. In chapters 1—43 we find groupings of proverbial (mainly two-line proverbs) sayings according to subject matter, often using word association and common topics to provide links. This shows an interesting difference from the book of Proverbs where the sayings tend to be more mixed up, although we do find in Ben Sira that the same theme is raised in more than one place and it is certainly not systematic (J. D. Harvey (1993) has recently argued for more order in the book than is usually supposed). Subjects include filial duty (Sir. 3:1–16); attitudes towards women (Sir. 9:1–9) (not always favourable! See Trenchard, 1982; Di Lella, 1995); the art of government (Sir. 9:7—10:18); and table manners (Sir. 31:12—32:13). More meditative passages in the form of poems, prayers and hymns preface and interrupt these sayings (Sir. 1—2; 24; 42:15—43:33), many of which reflect on the nature of wisdom and her relationship with God. This theme of the role of divine wisdom is expounded at greater length in chapters 44—50, in particular reference to the salvation history. The history of the fathers of Israel is expounded from Enoch through to the high priest of the author's own time (*c.* 180 BC), Simon, the son of Onias. B. L. Mack (1985) has suggested that this praise of worthy men is a charter ideology for the temple, forging national consciousness. Ben Sira has a clear familiarity with earlier scriptures and this may indicate that part of the scribal role by this time was in the preserving and handing down of sacred traditions. In chapter 51 we have an appendix consisting of a prayer, a psalm and an acrostic in autobiographical style, all seen as later additions. Evidence from Qumran which preserves this psalm as a separate piece in 11Q5 21–22 indicates that it had a separate existence. Ben Sira could well have been quoting an existent psalm or it could have been preserved as an extract from Ben Sira's book (see Chapter 11).

On the question of date, the first quarter of the second century BC (190–180 BC) is generally agreed upon by scholars (e.g. Skehan and Di Lella, 1987), although recently D. S. Williams (1994) has questioned this assumption, arguing for a date closer to 175 BC, on grounds of the supposed age-gap between the grandson who wrote the prologue in 132 BC and the grandfather, Ben Sira himself, an argument that is, in my view, somewhat tenuous. The earliest probable date for the book is 198 BC, the date set by the death of the high priest, Simon, the last of Ben Sira's famous men (Sir. 50:1–21). The latest is the beginning of the Hellenistic reform under Antiochus IV to which there is no reference in the book. Ben Sira is thought to have written in Jerusalem since he shows a close knowledge of the traditions of the Jerusalem temple (even seen as a Zadokite by J. F. A. Sawyer (1982) and as a proto-Sadducee by A. Di Lella (1966)). It has been pointed out however that there are links with Egyptian literature, for example with Papyrus Insinger, an Egyptian gnomic work written in demotic, which contains a similar ethic of caution based on shame and regard for one's name; c.f. Sirach 6:13; 13:1— 14:2; 29:20; 32:23; 41:11–13 (see J. T. Sanders (1983), opposed by M. Lichtheim (1983)). Whether this indicates direct Egyptian influence or simply an infiltration of ideas, it is also clear that Ben Sira was well travelled and so may have come into contact with a wider range of knowledge by this means.

There has been a great deal of debate whether, also on his travels, Ben Sira came into contact with Greek thought and thus how

We will now consider whether Ben Sira may be regarded as wisdom literature.

Form

Does Ben Sira contain the proverbial form basic to the wisdom literature? Ben Sira regularly uses the technique of the interpretation accompanying the proverb (e.g. Sirach 33:14–15; 39:33–4); but in Ben Sira the proverbial saying is a major form. It is hard to assess whether the proverbs that he uses are original or pre-existed in the tradition. Rarely does a proverb appear without an accompanying interpretation, and this certainly is an original feature. Often the author sets sayings concerning opposite issues alongside one another to provide contrasting descriptions, for example poverty and wealth in Sirach 13:3: 'A rich person does wrong, and even adds insults; a poor person suffers wrong, and must add apologies.' This resembles a pattern found in both Proverbs and Ecclesiastes. There is an interest in listing phenomena that we found in Proverbs, in Sirach 43, for example, where there is an appraisal of the wonders of nature (cf. Job 38), and in Sirach 38:24—39:11 in the listing of trades.

Does Ben Sira's book contain the autobiographical narrative? He uses the autobiographical genre once to show that his quest for wisdom was not only for himself (Sir. 33:16–18), but it is not a common genre in his work. Yet, even more than the other wisdom books, this book is a personal testimony. First, we know more about the author and his circumstances, and second, Ben Sira constantly gives us his own interpretation with the proverb he cites, and uses refrains for emphasis. The accompanying interpretation resembles a technique found in Ecclesiastes, although Ben Sira makes use of refrains more extensively and often uses them to link subject matter, e.g. Sirach 2:7–18, where three refrains are each used three times to link the topics under discussion. Some refrains use a technique of alternation, for example Sirach 7:22–4 where three questions occur, each followed by a word of advice. Others depend upon repetition of a single phrase: for example Sirach 6:14–16 uses 'a faithful friend' three times without juxtaposition with any other refrain. The trend towards prophecy found in Ben Sira is also a personal element, for, in the style of prophecy, the author personally exhorts the people, and warns and admonishes them to behave in the way he is advocating (Sir. 2:7–18).

What about a didactic element? We find this in the didactic essay and ancient debate forms (Sir. 15:11; cf. Eccl. 7:10), and in the didactic poetry. In fact, such genres abound in Ben Sira, e.g. poems about wisdom in Sirach 1:1–20 and 4:11–19, and poems about the creation of man in Sirach 16:24–30 and 17:1–12. M. Hengel remarks on Ben Sira's skill in using a great many poetical forms and writes: 'In this multiplicity he differs quite essentially from earlier wisdom; the multiplicity is an indication of the late form of this Hebrew poetry' ([1973] 1974, p. 131).

Prayers are very important in Ben Sira, e.g. Sirach 23:1–6. This is form which developed from small beginnings in the wisdom literature but does feature; e.g. in Proverbs. 30:7–9 we find a simple request for a balance between poverty and wealth. This resembles Ben Sira's appeal in 22:27—23:6, in which the refrain 'Lord, Father and Master of my life' is used in two direct requests accompanied by two indirect requests in Sirach 23:1 and 23:4. In Sirach 36:1–17 we find a lament familiar from the Psalter and in 51:1–12 a typical thanksgiving song. There may also have been a wider influence here from cultic circles.

We also find the hymn to wisdom form in Sirach 24:1–22, plus the general hymn form as found in the psalms in Sirach 42:15—43:33 (cf. Sir. 16:24—17:4; 39:12–35), not a form featured in earlier wisdom. We not only find cultic influence in Ben Sira but also the influence of prophecy or prophetic interests, in Sirach 24:30–4; 35:22–6 and 47:22 for example. This may indicate an overlapping of the roles of wise man and prophet in this period (Hengel, [1973] 1974; Baumgartner, 1914). Perhaps we can say more firmly that it represents the infiltration into wisdom literature of genres from outside mainstream wisdom, but that the link with prophecy is not new (see Chapter 6).

Content

On the issue whether or not there is an order to be found in the world, Ben Sira is more positive than Qoheleth. He asserts that all works of God are appropriate and that there is a fixed place for all things. He has a theory of opposites in which everything comes in pairs (e.g. male and female), and in which everything has its corresponding opposite. In Sirach 33:7–15, for example, the author contrasts holy days and ordinary days, and he contrasts the blessed and exalted with those who are cursed and brought low. He concludes in verse 15: 'Look at all the works of the Most High, they come in pairs, one the opposite of the other.'

Furthermore, Ben Sira asserts that human beings can know the right behaviour at the right time. It is the task of the wise person to realise the value of events and situations and choose the right option, although it is God who allocates the time, and human experience is not enough on its own to find it out. Unlike Qoheleth, human lack of knowledge about the proper time is not a negative thing; rather, God acts in every circumstance for good. In Sirach 39:16–35 he attacks those who believe they can judge the divine power as good or evil depending upon circumstances. In verse 33 Ben Sira writes: 'All the works of the Lord are good, and he will supply every need in its time.'

Ben Sira asserts that there are no limits to human knowledge so long as God is at the centre. Here we encounter the idea of God at the limits of wisdom, as found in Proverbs, accompanied by the idea of the availability of that wisdom through the appropriate channels. The fear of God is the beginning of wisdom (Sir. 1:16, 27) and is also linked with the observance of the Torah (Sir. 1:26; 6:37; 19:20; 21:11; 23:27). The precise nature of the relationship between these three concepts – fear of God, wisdom and Torah – has led to some scholarly debate, as I shall discuss below.

On the theme of the ambiguity of events, we find the same tension in Ben Sira as in Proverbs between self-reliance and the fear of God. Ben Sira advocates self-trust but adds a religious dimension to it which is the need to pray for divine guidance (Sir. 37:12–15). There is a divine realm which is not inaccessible to human beings, so that the cosmic entity of wisdom was grasped in the first place only by human effort. Rightful understanding of the benefits of wisdom can turn it from a burden to a beautiful bride (Sir. 6:18–31). In fact, Ben Sira enjoys contrasting things to heighten their ambivalence; for example, in 41:1–2 he shows how there are two sides to death, one bitter the other sweet: 'O death, how bitter is the thought of you to the one at peace among possessions, who has nothing to worry about and is prosperous in everything, and still is vigorous enough to enjoy food! O death, how welcome is your sentence to one who is needy and failing in strength, worn down by age and anxious about everything, to one who is contrary, and has lost all patience!' Although there is some airing of injustices in the manner of Qoheleth, such as that one person toils without success and achieves nothing whilst another who has no means or ability prospers (e.g. Sir. 11:11–12), there is mainly in this book a positive assessment of the seeming ambiguity of events. Such ambiguity does not prevent people from understanding and controlling their own lives as long as they are in close contact with God (Sir. 2:1–18). Unlike earlier wisdom, Ben Sira does not regard God as a limit imposed on human attempts to master life; rather, piety and a secure religious relationship with God are most important to this author. G. von Rad (1972) suggests a tendency towards pietism in Ben Sira. In contrast and in tension with earlier wisdom which taught that instruction was the means to wisdom, in Ben Sira to the pious man alone will wisdom be given, and thus faith is a necessity. Trust in God is so strong and confidence in the divine order so secure that not even contradictory experiences can shake the wise man. Ben Sira says of God in 2:6: 'Trust in him and he will help you: make your ways straight and hope in him.'

In the area of punishment and reward, there is in Ben Sira an emphasis on a right religious relationship as the goal of one's educational endeavours, and he encourages pious behaviour (Sir. 32:14–24). The wise person can discern right and wrong and can learn to make the right choices (Sir. 17:6f); and punishment and reward will be meted out justly by God. Although sometimes God's power seems to be hidden and God's logic is not evident in events, there is no doubting God's good intentions (e.g. Sir. 33:13–15). The idea of predestination also comes into play in that God is totally in control, and this sets up a conflict between predestination and human control over life by the choices made. For example, in Sir. 15:16 humans have to make the right choices in God's sight: 'He has placed before you fire and water; stretch out your hand for whichever you choose.'

The next theme was that of life as the supreme good. In Ben Sira the law is seen as the way to life. True wisdom is hidden in the Mosaic law which nonetheless does not restrict or replace traditional forms of wisdom teaching. Sacred history is also integrated into sapiential discourse (e.g. Sirach 44:1—50:21, the hymn in praise of the fathers which begins, 'Let us now sing the praises of famous men and our ancestors in their generations') as the means of revelation of that law. On the practical side, good actions have to be according to the law (Sir. 28:1–7), and since the law is from God, human beings must be in close communion with God to achieve their reward. Thus the emphasis, as in all wisdom, is on an individual's relationship with God but within a new framework of the overall authority of the law. There is no doubt that God is good (Sir. 33:13–15) and there is a positive assessment of the possibility of a positive relationship with God for each individual.

On the theme of confidence in wisdom, Ben Sira's positive confidence resembles that found in Proverbs, and yet in Ben Sira wisdom is quantitatively different: it is closely linked to the law and to the fear of God. It is interesting that the content of Ben Sira's wisdom does not change and take on a legalistic tone. Rather, it resembles traditional wisdom teaching and suggests that it is wisdom that is entering the remit of Torah rather than being ousted by it. The concept of the fear of God has likewise developed away from its simple meaning in Proverbs to express the need for fulfilment of ancient covenantal obligations expressed in the Torah (Sir. 1:26; 6:37; 19:20; 21:11; 23:27). And yet, this appeal is universal, a continuing characteristic of the wisdom quest.

On the final theme of the personification of wisdom, we find that in Ben Sira wisdom is linked with creation, notably the creation of the law which brought wisdom as appropriated by humans into being – here we see the cosmological and the anthropological in tension once again. The key text is Sirach 24:1–22 where we find wisdom who 'came forth from the mouth of the Most High' (Sir. 24:3), circuiting the heavens and earth and finding a resting place in Israel. We read in Sirach 24:8: 'He said, "Make your dwelling in Jacob, and in Israel receive your inheritance" ', and in verse 10, 'In the holy tent I ministered before him and so I was established in Zion.' Wisdom then finds a home in Israel where she can call to the people to respond to her. And the poem ends on this note: 'Whoever obeys me will not be put to shame, and those who work with me will not sin' (Sir. 24:22). Von Rad ([1970] 1972) comments that a line is drawn in Sirach 24 from the primeval order through to the revelation of Yahweh in temple and tabernacle, more of a cultic link than a salvation history link. Human response is, I would argue, a vital part of the fulfilment of the purpose of Wisdom, and the poem reflects this in its movement from God to humanity. In Ben Sira the human response is encapsulated in the Mosaic law. Wisdom, involved in creation, is even identified with the life-giving law which provides good for the devout and evil for sinners.

Context

This book contains its own superscription, describing itself as the Wisdom of Jesus, Ben Sira. We know nothing however of the specific contexts in which or for which it was written. It was originally composed in Hebrew in the second century BC. We have medieval manuscripts of it in Hebrew, and fragments found at Masada illustrate its status among Palestinian Jews of the first century AD. We also have evidence of its existence from Qumran (see below, Chapter 11). It is also perhaps the best known of the apocryphal books in the Christian Church, as its Latin title 'Ecclesiasticus' (Church Book) suggests. This book then is not attributed to Solomon but to an author – Jesus, Ben Sira – in 50:27: 'Instruction in understanding and knowledge I have written in this book, Jesus son of Eleazar son of Sirach of Jerusalem, whose mind poured forth wisdom.' This is the only wisdom book which is not attributed to a great hero of Israel's past (except Job), and hence a claim to actual authorship by this 'ostensible' author is strong. This change of technique to personal testimony rather than pseudonym may have been influenced by Hellenistic practice (Hengel, [1973] 1974).

We need to ask whether this book is likely to have a context in a school or teaching milieu, or whether it is sufficient to see it as a collection of instruction and knowledge which has drawn from a wider intellectual realm and is designed for a broader audience. It should be remembered that it is from Ben Sira that we have a description of the work of the wise man and the need for leisure (Sir. 38:24—39:11): 'How can one become wise who handles the plough . . . and whose talk is about bulls?' (v. 25). He describes the wise man as studying the law, as being knowledgeable about past wisdom and prophecies as well as the sayings of famous men and the intricacies of parables. The author is described as mixing with rulers and travelling abroad and he is also a man of prayer. This is a named work and has a personal touch that earlier wisdom literature lacks. The author may have been a priest as he shows some interest in cultic life and sacrifice and he praises the High Priest (for an alternative assessment of the evidence, see J. C. Snaith (1975) who argues that this is secondary to his concerns with social justice and personal devotion), or he may have been some kind of temple scribe. However, the prologue to the book by his grandson does suggest an educational context of some kind, albeit linked to study of the law:

> So my grandfather Jesus, who had devoted himself especially to the reading of the Law and the Prophets and the other books of our ancestors, and had acquired considerable proficiency in them, was himself also led to write something pertaining to instruction and wisdom, so that by becoming familiar also with his book those who love learning might make even greater progress in living according to the law.

J. L. Crenshaw (1997) has recently argued that the context of learning may well have been an oral one, since nowhere does Ben Sira mention the reading of texts or the doing of exercises in writing. Thus he imagines a verbal teaching situation. However, generally a more literary milieu is supposed and there is no reason why, along ancient Near Eastern lines, both oral and literary teaching methods may not have been practised.

R. N. Whybray (1974), in *The Intellectual Tradition in the Old Testament*, suggests that in the later period distinctions between groups of prophets, wise men and priests become more blurred and that there is more interrelationship between material. The combination of traditions found here would certainly support this

conclusion as would the words of Ben Sira's grandson in the prologue. The teaching milieu seems to have broadened its scope by
this period. This opening out of the wisdom tradition is described
by E. J. Schnabel as 'an identity in diversity' (1985, p. 91), and he
points to the particular relationship between wisdom and law in his
thought. This can be demonstrated in Ben Sira's concerns when we
start to unpack them in more detail.

Ben Sira's distinctive concerns

The two principal new features in Ben Sira are (a) allusions
to Israel's saving history and (b) the idea that true wisdom is hidden
in the Mosaic law.

Allusions to Israel's saving history

The first of these developments which sees Ben Sira in-
tegrating wisdom with the whole scheme of saving history has been
regarded as the final alignment of the wisdom tradition with mainline
Old Testament theology. We might however just as easily see the
lines of dependence the other way round – the time was now ripe
for wisdom to draft a scheme of world history into her creation ideas.
This had the effect of losing the universalism that characterised the
earlier wisdom enterprise, to make it more of a national product,
pertinent to Israel alone, and in fact boosting her claim to a special
place in God's plans and purposes, and hence a link with Israel's
saving history is a natural development.

So, in Ben Sira elements of saving history are woven with
universal ideas. The giving of the Torah is not just a historical event
from the time of the Exodus, rather it is traced back to creation (Sir.
24). It becomes equated with the divine principle of Wisdom
bestowed on the world at creation. It is God's divine call to humanity,
the means of revelation itself. Ben Sira expresses the doctrine that
Wisdom was created by Yahweh before any other creation. She came
forth from his mouth. All creation and every nation was open before
her, and she searched for a home on earth among human beings.
But her first attempt to find a habitation failed. God then assigned
her a resting place in Israel, and there, in the form of the Torah, she
took root and grew up into a magnificent tree. But Yahweh also left

a certain portion of wisdom possessed by the world outside Israel. Here the same Wisdom that makes the offer of salvation to the people of God is also designated as a teacher of the Gentiles. It is through her that they enjoy the blessings of law and order: all the wisdom of rulers derives from her. But, of course, only Israel can boast of the fullness of her gifts. This desire to clarify its own special place in the whole history of humankind – not just of Israel – probably sprang from Israel's being a vassal state in the Hellenistic age.

One way in which the saving history motifs are introduced in Ben Sira is through quotation of scripture. We begin to get the feeling with this book that the main period of authoritative scripture is now past – and it is certainly true that many of the books of the Old Testament would have been finalised and have come together as a group by this time. There is in Ben Sira a great interest in quotation of and allusion to scripture, even more so than in Ecclesiastes. We find a number of allusions from Pentateuchal traditions, notably from the primeval history in Genesis 1—11, for example Adam (Sir. 33:10; 40:1) and Eve (Sir. 25:24) and the tree of knowledge (Sir. 38:5); and in Sirach 16:24–30 and 17:1–12 Ben Sira retells the biblical account of the creation of humankind but with his own interpretation fusing with traditional ideas. He wants to say something about the intellectual relationship between humans and God, so he expresses awe at human intellectual equipment, notably at the ability to differentiate between good and evil (Sir. 17:6f). Since this issue is not actually mentioned in Genesis 1, on which Ben Sira's account is based, there is a need for interpretation. He thus reinterprets Genesis 1 from the viewpoint of knowledge of God's works and of the praise which humans owe to God for these. Other biblical allusions derive from elsewhere in the Pentateuch, for example the six hundred Israelites who perished in the wilderness (16:9–10) and the law of Moses (24:23), and some from sacred traditions, for example the holy Tabernacle, the special people of God in 24:1–12. This technique of quotation gives the book a sense of standing at the end of a tradition rather than creating a new one, and yet the old is used to forge new paths and fresh patterns of thought.

It is interesting to note that Ben Sira very much perceived himself as a traditionalist not as an innovator. For he says that he is determined by 'the discourse of the aged, for they themselves learned from their parents' (Sir. 8:9). He has a strong sense of the past and regards himself as the custodian of past traditions. Of course, it is possible that Ben Sira himself was not aware of the fact that he had developed the tradition which he had received. If he interpreted a book he probably read it entirely in the light of the presuppositions of his own day. Hence when he came to write down his own understanding of earlier material, it need not have appeared to him as new and innovative. His interpretation was how he had always interpreted, say, Proverbs, and in that sense he was maintaining the tradition.

Wisdom, law and the fear of God

The prominent place given to Torah in this book has led scholars such as J. L. Crenshaw (1982) to wonder whether in fact Ben Sira is moving away from the wisdom quest itself, since Torah really does not characterise that quest. Crenshaw also finds an accompanying interest in sacrifice and cultic life, complete performance of which is urged by Ben Sira (Sir. 35:4–11), as divergent from mainline wisdom thought, as indeed is Ben Sira's stress on piety in individual human behaviour. The law is thus the way to life, and Crenshaw sees wisdom in Ben Sira's thought as subordinated to it. It should be noted however that, despite a new emphasis on the Torah, Ben Sira's teaching has not become legalistic – traditional forms of wisdom teaching have not been replaced or restricted by legalism. Its main influence is that it engenders even more confidence in the wisdom quest. Crenshaw then subordinates the theme of wisdom in Ben Sira to the fear of God which includes adherence to the law.

Von Rad ([1970] 1972) on the other hand subordinates the theme fear of God to that of wisdom and plays down the emphasis on the law. He sees Ben Sira's interests in a different way. He argues that in the prologue in 1:1–10 Ben Sira presents wisdom as his major concern, not the fear of God, as is made clear in 50:27–9: 'Jesus the son of Eleazar son of Sirach of Jerusalem, whose mind poured forth wisdom' (v. 27b). Wisdom is used in this prologue to refer both to a primeval order outside human control (for example 1:4: 'Wisdom was created before all other things, and prudent understanding from eternity'), and to a wisdom which is needed by humanity but which human beings cannot acquire without the assistance of God: 'he lavished upon her those who love him' (v. 10b). Here we find the same tension between God's revelation and human acquisition of wisdom that we saw characterised the figure of Wisdom in Proverbs.

Ben Sira is also concerned with the fear of God which leads to wisdom. The idea that the fear of God is the beginning of all wisdom was in Proverbs 1—9 the basis of all search for knowledge; and Ben Sira repeats the statement in Sirach 1:14: 'To fear the Lord is the beginning of wisdom.' Von Rad argues however that for Ben Sira the phrase 'fear of God' needed much more explanation than it did for his predecessors. Proverbs assumes that people know what is meant by the fear of God – that is, reverence and obedience to the divine will – which Ben Sira also understands (Sir. 2:6; 32:14f). Ben Sira, however, broadens the concept, associating it with human experience (e.g. of joy in 1:11, and humility in 1:27), and aligning it with wisdom, for example Sirach 1:11f; 1:18, 20: 'To fear the Lord is the root of wisdom and her branches are long life' (v. 20); even at times identifying the fear of God with wisdom and instruction, e.g. Sirach 1:16 and 27: 'For the fear of the Lord is wisdom and discipline, fidelity and meekness are his delight' (v. 27). Above all, the fear of God is aligned with the Torah. But, von Rad argues that this does not divorce Ben Sira from the rest of wisdom thought. He writes: 'The didactic material presented by Ben Sira arises solely, as is abundantly clear, from didactic wisdom tradition and not from the Torah' ([1970] 1972, p. 244). He does not mean from this that the Torah does not play a part in Ben Sira's thought, but writes: 'It is simply a question of determining the theological point at which it exercises its specific function' (p. 244). This function is 'to give a more precise definition of and to clarify the idea of the fear of God' (p. 244). Von Rad finds evidence for this in the way in which the law always appears as an entity, 'the Torah' or 'the commandments' which has come to re-present God's divine will. Thus Ben Sira reinterprets the expression 'fear of God' for an age which heard God's voice through the Torah, e.g. Sirach 6:37: 'Reflect on the statutes of the Lord and meditate at all times on his commandments. It is he who will give insight to your mind, and your desire for wisdom will be granted.'

At times Ben Sira even makes a total identification of not only the fear of God with wisdom but of both of these with Torah, e.g. Sirach 19:20: 'The whole of wisdom is the fear of the Lord, and in all wisdom there is the fulfilment of the law' (cf. Sir. 21:11 and 23:27). However, the fear of God was not solely inspired by the Torah; observation of the works of creation also leads humans to the fear of God as in Sirach 43 (Haspecker, 1967). Von Rad argues therefore that Torah is just one new step towards defining the fear of God. The functions of wisdom have not been replaced by Torah; rather, they have been enhanced by the inclusion of Torah. Thus Torah is of relevance only where it is connected with wisdom teachings. Von Rad writes of Sirach 24, the didactic poem concerning primeval wisdom: 'Notice that it is wisdom who speaks here, not Torah, and this is where Sirach's heart beats. Primeval wisdom is here regarded as a fascinating, aesthetic phenomenon. Where Torah is concerned, Sirach does not rise to such enthusiastic statements' ([1970] 1972, p. 246). Von Rad thus successfully shows how the interest in Torah is a natural progression of existing ideas from within wisdom thinking rather than an abandonment of the distinctive wisdom quest.

Concluding remarks

We find in Ben Sira a broadening of concerns and a much wider influence from other areas of Israelite life, and yet we are still able to call it wisdom literature. We see a development in wisdom ideas, and yet one which is essentially in harmony with what went before. It contains proverbial wisdom, but usually with an accompanying interpretation in the manner of the author of Ecclesiastes (e.g. Sir. 33:14–15; 39:33–4). Ben Sira uses a style of exhortation that resembles prophecy and uses refrains for emphasis. He also uses poetry, hymn forms (especially hymns to wisdom) and prayers, and so there is a real mix of genres in his work which stretches the boundaries of a narrow definition of wisdom.

9: THE WISDOM OF SOLOMON

For she [Wisdom] is a breath of the power of God, and a
pure emanation of the glory of the Almighty. (Wisd. 7:25)

In the Wisdom of Solomon the wisdom element, that of
discussion of the theological implications of humanity in
relationship with God, is merged with historical concerns regarding
Israelite history and the election of the chosen people, and religious
concerns such as polemic against idols, as well as theological concerns such as repentance. With the Wisdom of Solomon we have a
wisdom book of a rather different character which starts to strain
our definition of what wisdom is, and yet there are sufficient similarities to be able to see it as a legitimate development within the
wisdom category.

Date and setting

The Wisdom of Solomon, written in the Greek language, is
most probably a first-century BC work, widely thought to have been
produced in Egypt and influenced by Greek ideas (see below). A
range of dates of composition have been suggested from the third
century BC to the second century AD (Larcher, 1983–5). The most
common first-century BC date narrows the composition down further
to the period after 47 BC, the Roman conquest of Egypt, on the
grounds of references to persecution and idolatry and the presence
of late vocabulary in the book. This would date the book around 30
BC in the reign of Augustus which is the preferred view among
scholars. D. Winston (1979), on the other hand, has revived an older
idea of a first-century AD setting at the time of the Emperor Caligula
(see Goodrick, 1913), which has won some support. An Egyptian
setting for composition has received wide support from scholars on
the grounds that there is a good deal of anti–Egypt polemic (e.g.
Wisd. 19:13–17; Zimmerman, 1966–7). Alexandria was a major centre
for Jews and it is clear from the book that by this time the earlier
optimism of the Alexandrian Jewish community for a meeting of
cultures and social acceptance of them had been replaced by growing

disappointment, reflected in the criticism of pagan culture contained in the book. J. M. Reese (1970) argues that the Wisdom of Solomon is addressed to the Jewish youth in Alexandria, largely to counter their inclination towards Isis worship. He argues that the author draws on features of the Isis cult of ancient Egypt, using imagery of the goddess Isis to describe Wisdom (see also Mack, 1973). A close link with Isis worship is rejected by other scholars (e.g. J. S. Kloppenburg, 1982), but the idea of Jewish youths being the audience, a group attracted by Hellenisation while tempted to reject their ancestral faith, has found some support. However, it may be more plausible that it is the whole of Jewish society in Alexandria that is being addressed. Another alternative is that a Graeco-Roman audience was also in mind. While the discussion of God's contrasting judgement on Israel and Egypt (chapters 10—19) seems to be more directed at a Jewish audience, the detailed attack on idolatry and the exhortations to kings and rulers may be directed to a Gentile audience. However, this is likely to be a secondary concern.

Hellenistic influence

There is some debate as to the extent of Hellenistic influence on the Wisdom of Solomon. There is a clear exhortatory style in the book with lyrical poetry and philosophical argument, praise of wisdom and denunciations of the heathen giving it a unique character. The echoes in the book of Greek philosophies and the use of technical Greek terms, combined with the evidence of quotation of scripture from the Septuagint (Isa. 3:10 in Wisd. 2:12; Isa. 44:20 in Wisd. 15:10 and Job 9:12, 19 in Wisd. 12:12), all indicate that it is a Greek production. As for literary influence, J. M. Reese (1970) divides the Wisdom of Solomon into four sections each corresponding to a different Hellenistic 'small literary genre'. He then argues that the Hellenistic genre encompassing all these smaller genres is the 'protreptic' – a type of philosophical rhetoric – or didactic exhortation. The aim of this kind of exhortation was to seek to persuade others to pursue a course of action both by appeal to the intellect and by the use of rhetoric. This incorporated elements of diatribe, the popular moral invective characteristic of the Hellenistic period. This discussion is part of a wider debate about genre, another suggestion being that of the encomium, another Greek genre which rather than encouraging action, is primarily aimed at persuading listeners to admire something and ultimately adopt it (P. Beauchamp, 1975). J. M. Reese (1970) argues that this writer probably thought in Greek categories but used primarily Jewish traditions. L. L. Grabbe (1997) has recently argued that the Wisdom of Solomon (chs. 10–19 in particular) is best seen as a Hellenised Jewish midrash given its extensive allusion to biblical texts. There is opposition to such views, from D. Winston (1979), who denies Hebraic sources for the book and there were older scholars (e.g. P. Heinisch, 1908) who saw the thought of the Wisdom of Solomon as substantially identical with that of the Old Testament, hardly recognising the presence of any Greek philosophy.

On the issue of Greek influence, the author clearly had contact with Greek culture, literature and philosophy, but that he actually espoused any one formal philosophical system is unlikely. The fresh developments in his presentation of the female figure of Wisdom in particular are thought to have been influenced by Stoic ideas of logos and pneuma which also influenced Philo. Wisdom bestows on sages the four cardinal virtues of self–control, intelligence, justice and courage (Wisd. 8:7), a classification that goes back to Plato and was taken up by Zeno, founder of the Stoic school. There is probably also an influence in the book from Middle Platonism, particularly in ideas of the soul and hints at the concept of immortality, e.g. in Wisdom 2:23 which speaks of human beings created in 'the image of his [God's] own eternity'. It is perhaps most likely that he picked up ideas from wandering teachers of philosophy who spoke about it in the market places. As A. T. S. Goodrick wrote in 1913, 'the student must be warned that he will find in Pseudo-Solomon no exact philosophical reasoner, but rather a loose rhetorical thinker who uses the first word that comes to hand . . .' (p. 48). There is clearly a meeting of Jewish and Hellenistic thought by this period, to which the author of the Wisdom of Solomon witnesses, an outlook that appears at a deeper level in Philo and is part of the background of the New Testament and the developments in early Christian thinking.

Outline

The book naturally divides into a number of sections. The first section is chapters 1—5, a discourse on righteousness and wickedness addressed to the 'rulers of the earth' (Wisd. 1:1), who are encouraged to pursue justice or wisdom while admonishing those whose behaviour will result in destruction. The just are promised ultimate vindication and immortality among the angels of heaven, in contrast to the frightening judgement of the wicked. The second section is chapters 6—9 on the figure of wisdom, with Solomon as the speaker telling the mighty of the earth to 'get wisdom'. The third section, in chapters 10—19, is a midrash on God's activities in history, with wisdom in prominent place. The history of Israel from Adam to the conquest of Canaan is surveyed, a history punctuated by references to idol-worship, this being the main section of diatribe against the Egyptians, recalling the Exodus period in particular. This structure is widely agreed for the book, although some divide the second section at chapter 10 and start the third at chapter 11. Recent scholars have pursued more complex breakdowns of the book, some arguing for a breakdown into four sections (J. M. Reese), others having been interested in the phenomenon of parallelism in the book (A. G. Wright (1967) who argued for a concentric pattern in different sections of the book). The book is widely agreed nowadays to be a structured unity, as many Greek writings are, although this was not the opinion of older scholars, especially among those who saw parts of the book (notably chapters 1—5 on grounds of different subject matter) as having a Hebrew or Aramaic original (Purinton, 1928; Zimmerman, 1966–7).

We need to decide next whether we can really include the Wisdom of Solomon as wisdom literature, with the awareness that wisdom is becoming less and less of a separate phenomenon, and second, as with Ben Sira, we need to consider what the distinctive concerns of this author are.

Form

There is relatively little evidence of proverbial or instruction material in the Wisdom of Solomon. There is a list in Wisdom 7:17–20 where the author alludes to the entire curriculum of the wise man in the manner of lists found in Proverbs and Ben Sira: 'For it is he who gave me unerring knowledge of what exists, to know the structure of the world and the activity of the elements; the beginning and end and middle times, the alternations of the solstices and the changes of the seasons.' There are also lists of virtues and vices in Wisdom 14:22–31. Wisdom has now become knowledge of secrets, especially cosmic secrets as evidenced in apocalyptic works such as Daniel and Enoch.

Can we find autobiographical narrative here in the Wisdom of Solomon? As in Ben Sira there are warnings and admonitions in a semi–prophetic style (e.g. Wisd. 2:1–20 and 5:3–13) which show, according to J. L. Crenshaw, similarities to the 'imagined speech' form found in Proverbs (1:19; 1:22–23) but there is no direct autobiographical narrative. Crenshaw writes: 'In each case the musings of wicked men are brought to light, together with the warning that such reasoning leads to destruction' (1974, p. 69). This later period finds those who wrote any books learned in 'scripture' in general, including the prophetic books whose style they were by now versatile enough to imitate.

In the area of didactic poetry, we find that in general the Wisdom of Solomon contains poetry of a more imaginative type. There is a tendency towards prayers and psalms: for example, Wisdom 9:1–18 where we find a prayer form, and Wisdom 11:21—12:27, a broken prayer form. It is curious that the literary style of the book varies from poetic patches of high lyrical quality to plodding pedestrian prose.

There is evidence in the Wisdom of Solomon of the hymn to wisdom genre. The Wisdom of Solomon praises wisdom and describes her nature and works in a similar style to Ben Sira (i.e., in two hymns to wisdom, in Wisd. 6:12–20 and 7:22—8:21). Here the influence of Greek rhetoric was seen by Augustine in 6:17–20, and Greek influence posited for the list of attributes in 7:22–3 and cardinal virtues in 8:7 assigned to the figure of Wisdom.

On the level of form therefore we can see the closest similarities to Ben Sira within wisdom literature and yet we find the forms to be quite dissimilar to Proverbs, with the exception of the hymn to Wisdom, which reflects the fact that this motif is considerably more developed here. We can also see the influence of ideas from a different thought world which makes our classifications even more complex.

Content

On the first theme of order in the world, we find in this book the same emphasis on God as we found in Ben Sira. This is found in the context of a discussion of the theological implications of humanity's relationship with God. For example, the stress on God's mercy in Wisdom 3:9 in a refrain which occurs twice, 'grace and mercy are upon his holy ones and he watches over his elect', although note here the emphasis on the elect and loss of former universalism. Another example is emphasis on God's divine foreknowledge (Wisd. 7:7–8) and on his forebearance which, in its delaying of punishments, leads people to question whether God really does maintain justice in the universe. Such questioning leads some to a lifestyle in which sensual gratification becomes the highest good and this the Wisdom of Solomon strongly attacks, for example in Wisdom 1:16—2:24. Such concerns also lead him to condemn other human perversions such as idol worship in Wisdom 13:1—15:19: 'For the worship of idols not to be named is the beginning and cause and end of every evil' (Wisd. 14:27). As in Ben Sira, the distinctively 'wisdom' element is merged with historical concerns regarding Israelite history and the election of the chosen people; with religious concerns such as the polemic against idols; and with theological concerns such as repentance.

The ambiguity of events is by this stage lost in a more dogmatic scheme of a relationship between God and human beings in which contradictory experiences can be explained away in the context of knowledge of the divine nature and purpose. The polemic against idols, for example, draws out the contradiction between worshipping a dead thing instead of worshipping the creator God. The message here is that worship of the creation without the creator is a vain pursuit.

On the topic of punishment and reward, in the Wisdom of Solomon there is confidence in the beneficial effects of correct human behaviour which is expressed in the warnings against pride, as familiar from Proverbs (e.g. Prov. 25:6). In the Wisdom of Solomon the godless have reached a state of self-knowledge that is unhealthy and leads nowhere (e.g. Wisd. 5:8f). There is also the idea that virtue is always better than vice. An example of the stress on virtue is the way the Wisdom of Solomon extends the old maxim that progeny is an indication of God's favour to include barren women (Wisd. 3:13; 4:1) and eunuchs (Wisd. 3:14) as long as they are virtuous (cf. Isaiah 56:3–4). Creation itself fights on behalf of the righteous (Wisd. 5:15–23; 16:17; 16:24). Virtue includes full faith in God (Wisd. 1:2–5), a theological emphasis also found in Ben Sira. It is clear that there can be no reward without faith in God.

The next theme is that of life as the supreme good. Good and evil are seen as very real forces linked theologically with the creative wisdom of the spirit and with the frail sphere of the spirit. There is a detailed description of all the terrors and hallucinations which assailed the enemies of the people of God 'shut up in a prison not made of iron' (Wisd. 17:16), a prison of their own anxieties (Wisd. 17:17–21). Von Rad ([1970] 1972) argues that in the Wisdom of Solomon the world is for the first time divided into a benevolent one ruled by God and a malevolent one ruled by evil. Death does not come from God; rather, it came into the world through the envy of the devil (Wisd. 1:13; 2:24). M. Kolarcik (1991) writes on the author's preoccupation with death and the importance of this theme in the book. A life well lived has as its reward the attainment of advanced years as we read in Wisdom 4:8–9: 'For old age is not honoured for length of time, or measured by number of years; but understanding is grey hair for anyone, and a blameless life is ripe old age.'

Turning to the theme of confidence in wisdom, we find that this features considerably here. However, in the Wisdom of Solomon there is a new emphasis on the community of the elect (Wisd. 3:9; 15:2: 'but we will not sin, because we know that you acknowledge us as yours' (v. 2b)). A wide experiential knowledge is no longer valued as highly as it was. Rather, knowledge is acquired by means of faith in God and hence is available only to the elect. This is a marked change from the universalism that characterised earlier wisdom, and yet there are moments when the author realises that since no one can limit God or call him to account, ideas of election cannot be fully defended (Wisd. 12:12–18). There are tensions apparent in his work. God's saving purpose is directed at all the righteous everywhere, for example in 3:1 all the souls of the righteous (not just the elect) rest in God's hand; this idea is in tension with the desire to confirm the special relationship of Israel with God. Furthermore, the possibility of God acting on behalf of others is raised in Wisdom 11:15–20 where lenience is granted to the Egyptians; and this is in tension with God's unique concern for Israel as demonstrated in their saving history.

The personification of wisdom has a very important place for this author. By the time of the Wisdom of Solomon the concept pervades all wisdom thinking and the assessment of the value of the wisdom exercise. There is a very rich imagery of wisdom displayed here, which clearly has it roots in earlier wisdom. Here, however, wisdom is hypostatised rather than merely personified. A 'hypostasis' is defined by W. O. E. Oesterley and G. H. Box as 'a quasi–personification of certain attributes proper to God, occupying an intermediate position between personalities and abstract beings' (1911, p. 169). There is particular interest in Wisdom's relationship to God. She is the manifestation of God to humans, an emanation of divine attributes. In Wisdom 7:22 we read: 'for wisdom, the fashioner of all things, taught me. There is in her a spirit that is intelligent, holy, unique, manifold, subtle, mobile, clear, unpolluted, distinct, invulnerable, loving the good, keen, irresistible.' She is the orderer and creator of all things (Wisd. 8:1, 6). She is the teacher of virtues such as self–control and justice (Wisd. 8:7), and the supplier of all instruction (Wisd. 7:17–22), including information on branches of the natural sciences. This poem is presented as an exposition of what Wisdom taught the author. It begins with a cosmological description of Wisdom's relationship to God. It speaks of her action in creation and her superiority to all created things in her ordering role. Then the author goes on in 8:2 to describe his own relationship to her. Wisdom is there to teach her followers to respond to her, and this the author does: 'I loved her and sought her from my youth.' There then follows in 8:3–16 a description of what Wisdom can give to those who respond to her – knowledge, riches, understanding, righteousness, experience – her benefits cannot be surpassed. Here I would argue that we find the same interplay between God and humanity that we have found in other hymns to wisdom – the essential relation-ship of wisdom is found in this dialogue.

Clearly, the content of this work has much in common with other wisdom literature, especially Ben Sira, but again it is a far cry from Proverbs, except in its interest in the figure of Wisdom. Our classification of wisdom literature is being strained to its limits and yet, while the Wisdom of Solomon belongs more to wisdom than to any other genre, the varied forms and content of the book can be seen as evidence of the breaking down of distinctions between the classifications of wisdom, prophecy, cult and so on.

Context

This work is attributed to Solomon and yet it is from a period much later than the time in which Solomon lived, and on grounds of chronology alone therefore could not have been written by him. The book was probably attributed to Solomon as the symbol of the greatest wisdom thinker, to add more weight to the content of the book in characteristic pseudonymous style. It does however have a wider religious context than just a wisdom one with interests in prophecy in particular, and it shows tendencies that indicate that the people of God are now an oppressed minority, a vassal state of succeeding great empires. We probably need to include it as wisdom literature but we are aware that wisdom is becoming less distinctive and is increasingly to be seen in conjunction both with influences from other areas of Israelite life and also from outside Israelite culture.

Distinctive concerns of the author

New aspects of the figure of Wisdom

Clearly at the centre of concern in this book is the figure of Wisdom. There is much that is new about this image in the Wisdom of Solomon. Even Sirach 24 adds little by comparison to the Wisdom of Solomon. According to von Rad, this author abandons the line which had been adhered to up until this point and takes a decisive step along the road to what von Rad calls 'a mythical, specu-lative deification of wisdom' ([1970] 1972, p. 170). He points out that this transformation has been largely caused by the new use of Greek terminology by the author, for example in 1:6 Wisdom is 'spirit', she is a 'breath' of the power of God, an 'emanation' of the power of the Almighty (Wisd. 7:25), which has been made here into a hypostasis, rather than simply a personification of certain attributes. Wisdom is still in an intermediary role although she is identified more strongly with the divine.

There is a close relationship between wisdom and prophecy emerging in this book. Wisdom herself is also that which enters holy souls and makes them into prophets (Wisd. 7:27). She is also the source of all human wisdom: she is portrayed as Solomon's bride who enables him to rule wisely and justly, and yet at the same time she is God's bride and controls all the events of Israel's past and present. She guided the chosen people from the very·beginning; the final ten chapters (10—19) consist largely of a midrashic exposition on the Exodus experience. Von Rad sees the Wisdom of Solomon, in the way in which it uses old historical traditions, as very close to apocalyptic. He writes: 'In both, history has become teaching material from which one can derive, with comparative ease, knowledge for the present' ([1970] 1972, p. 283). History acquires a determinism that enables life in the present to be fully understood. Unlike prophecy, in which the possibility of change of the course of events through repentance is always kept open, in this view of history this option is gone. Furthermore, a link with apocalyptic is found in the way that the author of the Wisdom of Solomon acknowledges that the knowledge of all earthly phenomena comes from God – the knowledge of the cycles of the year, of the stars, of the differences between plants and the virtues of roots (Wisd. 7:15f). He is referring to branches of knowledge here. In Wisdom 8:7b, eight practical aspects of wisdom are mentioned – for example training in composure, understanding and justice. Then however there are mentioned areas of knowledge – the science of omens, interpretation of the future – which accrued secondarily to the wise only in the latest period and has come to be known as 'mantic wisdom', again with an influence on the interest in the magical we find in apocalyptic (see Chapter 11).

Another area of development of the Wisdom concept is in its interest in intellectual love, that is the question of the relationship between humanity and wisdom immanent in the world. This is the side of wisdom turned to human beings, thus maintaining the cosmo-logical/anthropological tension so essential to this figure and to wisdom itself. Wisdom, that mysterious order in the world, not only addresses humankind; it also loves human beings, and the motif of love-language spreads out widely in the texts. These ideas have developed from earlier wisdom: in Proverbs wisdom is a woman in the street wooing her hearers; in the Wisdom of Solomon the teachers speak in the style of biographical confessions, of wisdom's wooing and of the wonderful success of her efforts (Wisd. 8:2, 16; cf. Sir. 51:13, 19, 26f). There is thus a sublime bond of love between human beings and the divine mystery of creation. In the Wisdom of Solomon the human desire for wisdom meets a Wisdom that is already reaching out for humankind (Wisd. 6:12–16; cf. Sir. 15:2).

Polemic against idols

Polemic against idols features prominently in the Wisdom of Solomon and is seen to be a new element in wisdom, probably included under the influence of prophetic interests. Von Rad argues however that at least some of the ideas expressed on this subject have no real novelty in wisdom thought. For example, he says that the argument in Wisdom 13:1–9 that the worship of images is foolish, because the true creator can be recognised in what he has created, fits in with the doctrine of the self-revelation of creation found, for example, in Proverbs 8. The author of the Wisdom of Solomon sees idol worship as the cause and end of all evil, e.g. in Wisdom 14:27: 'For the worship of idols not to be named is the beginning and cause and end of every evil.' He condones the worship of nature since God is manifest in all created things, but he condemns the worship of creation without the creator, that is, the worship of lifeless objects, e.g. Wisdom 13:18: 'For health he appeals to a thing that is weak; for life he prays to a thing that is dead; for aid he entreats a thing that is utterly inexperienced; for a prosperous journey, a thing that cannot take a step.' Von Rad studies polemic against idols in the prophets and in the Wisdom of Solomon and notes a marked difference in their treatments, the reason for which he attributes largely to the Hellenistic Jewish influence. In the Wisdom of Solomon the folly of worshipping images is a main theme and its airing is not without a touch of irony, e.g. Wisdom 14:1: 'Again, one preparing to sail and about to voyage over raging waves calls upon a piece of wood more fragile than the ship which carries him.' Von Rad argues that the treatment here is more refined than in the prophets. Two types of people are considered here. There are those who see the elements as gods, when they should have recognised the Creator in what he created, and so, in that sense, they are guilty. Yet they are exonerated by the fact that at least they are searching for God, a positive point in their favour. It is those who worship something man-made that is lifeless who are morally degenerate (e.g. Wisd. 13:10–19). Von Rad writes on this: 'Since these images do not have the status of gods, they are, of course, also incapable of keeping men in the true fear of God (14:12, 23–31)' ([1970] 1972, p. 183).

Concluding remarks

The Wisdom of Solomon is, like Ben Sira, more positive wisdom. Some of the issues of earlier wisdom previously expressed in a negative way appear here in a more positive light. For example, the negative attitude towards old age found in Ecclesiastes is now replaced by an attitude which sees the attainment of advanced years as a reward for a life well lived, e.g. Wisdom 4:8: 'For old age is not honoured for length of time, nor measured by number of years.' Ideas of God and the Devil start to come in to explain away many of the earlier problems of theodicy. Wisdom has by this stage incorporated into it a theological framework with links with Persian dualism and Greek thought from outside Israelite thought, and with prophecy and salvation history from within it, all of which enable it to counter much that vexed the early wisdom writers. The Wisdom of Solomon is wisdom made palatable to a distinctive religious tradition which retains some of the characteristics of its earlier wisdom counterparts, but which loses much of the uniqueness of that tradition which kept it a separate strand of biblical theology. It is wisdom literature in that wisdom developed in this direction, but it is a much less distinctive wisdom tradition that we now encounter which strains the definition to its limit.

10: WISDOM'S WIDENING NET

You will never become wise if you think you are wise before you are. (*Sentences of Sextus* 199)

The broadening and development of wisdom leads us again into further problems of definition when we look at other books or sections of books which might have a claim to be called wisdom. We have seen how the Wisdom of Solomon stretched our definition to its limits. It is probably better as we turn to further diverse works that have connections with wisdom genres to speak of wisdom influence rather than wisdom literature because of the ever diversifing nature of outside influences upon wisdom and because of the, by now, fragile nature of the definition. In this chapter we will consider material from the Apocrypha, from the Pseudepigrapha, from early Jewish writings and from the Sentences of Phocylides from the Greek world.

The Apocrypha

1 Esdras 3:1—5:3

J. L. Crenshaw (1982) argues, on the basis of similarities primarily with Ben Sira, for a direct relationship between wisdom literature and the late historiographical work 1 Esdras 3:1—5:3, a story which tells of a contest between Darius the Mede's guards. He thus wants to include it as wisdom literature, also finding some similarities with the book of Ecclesiastes. Analogies have also been made between this work and the Egyptian Instruction of Ptahhotep (notably the final praise of truth in 1 Esdras 4:38–42; cf. Ptahhotep 510f). On the level of form the passage is largely composed of narrative, but certainly not on the narrative level of Job. There are overtones of short passages in Ecclesiastes (e.g. polarities used in 1 Esdras 4:7–9 and Ecclesiastes 3:1–9), but the similarities are not extensive. Its main genre seems to be a more historical one, with some signs of the influence of wisdom themes. On the level of content the link with wisdom is more obvious: there are signs of experiential wisdom, e.g. in the warnings against drunkenness (1 Esdras 3:18–24; cf. Proverbs 20:1–2; 23:29–35); and there is exploration of more profound themes such as the stress on eternal truth which has overtones of Ben Sira (1 Esdras 4:37–8; Sirach 17:31–2) and praise of the sun (1 Esdras 4:34; Sirach 43:5). The context would seem to be a court setting, since the material concerns the king and his courtiers, and those wishing to place wisdom in a court setting often emphasise this narrative. It seems likely to have been an anecdote which has found its way into a fresh setting, a didactic purpose being part of the story, but with historical and theological factors also playing a part. It is another piece that cuts across the genres, a characteristic of later material.

Baruch 3:9—4:4

Another contender is Baruch 3:9—4:4, a hymn in praise of wisdom which draws heavily on images and concepts from wisdom hymns in Proverbs, Job and Ben Sira. The form of the passage is similar to other wisdom literature, such as Ben Sira, since it is a hymn to wisdom; and it even resembles hymns in the Psalter. As far as content is concerned, similar themes to other wisdom texts are apparent – especially to Job 28 (cf. Deut. 30:12–14) and Sirach 24. In Baruch 3:30 we read of Wisdom: 'Who has gone over the sea, and found her, and will buy her for pure gold?' So in Job 28:14 we read: 'The deep says, "It is not in me," and the sea says, "It is not with me." ' There is an invitation to Israel to remain faithful to the Torah, which is the path of wisdom, an identification that is becoming familiar in this period. Crenshaw writes: 'As a consequence of extensive reliance upon earlier texts, this hymn signals no advance in sapiential reflection' (1982, p. 187), and there is a sense in which this work follows the increasing tendency to quote scripture and recycle its images. Yet in Baruch 3:37 we might argue for originality in the idea that Wisdom lived among humankind, a sentiment that takes the personification of wisdom one step further than Proverbs, and even beyond the particularity of Ben Sira and the Wisdom of Solomon. Because of the brevity of the passage it is difficult to assign a date or context to this hymn; it may shed interesting further light on the relationship between wisdom and cult and be the product of Temple circles, roughly contemporary with Ben Sira.

Tobit

Tobit links up to wisdom literature through its references to the Wisdom of Ahikar (see chapter 7). For example, Tobit 4 gives Tobit's testament in the form of a counsel or maxims, some of which are taken exactly from Ahikar. Ahikar is mentioned in Tobit 1:21–2:

> [He is] the son of my brother, Hanael, over all the accounts of his kingdom, and he had authority over the entire administration. Ahikar interceded for me, and I returned to Nineveh. Now Ahikar was chief cupbearer, keeper of the signet, and in charge of administrations of the accounts under King Sennacherib of Assyria, so Esarhaddon reappointed him. He was my nephew and so a close relative.

He is also mentioned in Tobit 2:10; 11:18 and 14:10. The main section that parallels the content of the wisdom literature is 4:1–21, a section of moral teaching. The idea that good behaviour leads to prosperity is found: 'for those who act in accordance with truth will prosper in all their activities' (v. 6a); and there are warnings against pride and exhortations for fair dealing with one's employees (v. 14). There are warnings against drinking to excess: 'Do not drink wine to excess or let drunkenness go with you on your way' (v. 15b); and advice to consult the wise for counsel on any matter (v. 18). There is the ideal of giving to the poor in verses 7–11 and 16, an emphasis found in later wisdom such as Sirach 3:30, and an emphasis on prayer (v. 19) also found in the later wisdom books. The section also contains more particular advice, however, about taking a wife from within one's own tribal group (vv. 12–13), which is outside the concerns of wisdom literature, although warnings against a foreign woman have an air of familiarity (cf. the strange woman of Proverbs 9).

The Pseudepigrapha

Enoch

This is a pseudepigraphic work and an apocalyptic one also. Wisdom elements may be traced particularly in 1 Enoch in the picture of wisdom looking for a place to live and finally choosing, not Jerusalem, as in Ben Sira, but heaven among the angels. We read in 42:1-2: 'Wisdom could not find a place in which she could dwell; but a place was found [for] her in the heavens. Then Wisdom went out to dwell with the children of the people, but she found no dwelling place. [So] Wisdom returned to her place and she settled permanently among the angels' (Charlesworth, 1983, p. 33). The praise of wisdom is a favourite theme in this book. She dwells in heaven and came down among human beings, and yet no place could be found for her because of the evil treatment of her by them. She will return in the future: 'And then there shall be bestowed upon the elect wisdom, And they shall all live and never again sin.' There is a new emphasis here on an elect group and on wisdom's revelation of hidden secrets to this group within the broader scheme of world history. There is an interest in astromonical secrets: for example, the lightnings and stars of heaven are weighed in a righteous balance according to their proportions of light. The genre of this material is clearly apocalyptic rather than wisdom, although it shows how wisdom thought entered into all spheres of Israelite literature including its speculation about the future. The material has probably been influenced by wisdom ideas but is so fragmentary that it cannot be counted as wisdom literature.

Early Rabbinic interpreters

Pirke Aboth

In rabbinic literature, parts of the Mishnah, such as the Pirke Aboth (second century AD), have links with biblical wisdom and show influence of wisdom ideas. The Pirke Aboth contains many maxims and ethical sayings in similar vein to Proverbs and Ben Sira, e.g. I. 7: 'Nittai the Arbelite said, "Keep far from the evil neighbour and consort not with the wicked, and be not doubtful of retribution." ' It is interesting here that maxims are attributed to individuals rather than being in a more abstract formulation and rather than the whole work being attributed to an author. We also find sequential maxims which are not a feature of proverbial wisdom literature: 'He used to say... Moreover, he saw a skull which floated on the face of the water, and he said...' (II. 6, 7.) and a number of the mainline forms of wisdom literature are not present. H. A. Fischel (1975) argues, as part of a wider discussion of wisdom's influence and role in midrashic material, that the aims of Pirke Aboth, which differ from those of biblical wisdom, are first to establish a chain of tradition, from teacher to pupil, and second to introduce important teachings and opinions of philosophers, jurists and physicians. He then launches into a discussion of Western influence upon Pirke Aboth which provides, he maintains, a more appropriate milieu for the work than biblical wisdom does.

Here we find extensive quotation of scripture to add weight to an ethical saying and in particular quotation of Torah. In fact, the wise man is the one who adheres to Torah, as in Ben Sira, but Ben Sira also sees wisdom in many other categories whereas here it is restricted to Torah alone. There is no glorification of wisdom as an entity itself or as an attribute of God. In III. 21 we read:

> R. Eleazar ben Azariah said: – 'If there is no Torah there is no worldly occupation, and if there be no worldly occupation there is no Torah. If there is no wisdom there is no fear and if there is no fear there is no wisdom. If there is no knowledge there is no understanding, and if there is no understanding there is no knowledge. If there is no meal there is no Torah, if there is no Torah, there is no meal.'

Wisdom remains pragmatic, even in its latest formulations. Yet there are links made also with the cosmological side of wisdom: study of the law links up with God's purpose for the world and humanity, of which Israel is the witness. There is interest in the afterlife and judgement (in chapters III—IV) as well as interest in wise behaviour and the study of the law (chapters I—II). For example, in I. 17 'Simeon his son said: "All my days I have grown up among the Wise, and I have not found anything better for one than silence; and not study is the chief thing but action; and whoso multiplies words occasions sin."' This suggests that the wise were a particular social group at this time. However, in view of the close links between wisdom and Torah by this stage, such a class of men could well be synonymous with the class of Rabbis who interpreted the law and used their wisdom in so doing. Chapter V of the work draws on wider biblical history and draws a picture of a faithful disciple, making links between biblical history, wisdom and Torah as the later wisdom books do.

Hellenistic influence on works of wisdom

The Sentences of Phocylides

What makes the content of these Sentences interesting is the fact that 'the ethics and wisdom of Israel here encounter those of pagan Hellenism' (Gilbert, 1984, p. 316). While half of the sentences have parallels in Greek maxims (van der Horst, 1978), there is much that resembles Israelite wisdom thought. The first groups of sayings are inspired by the Decalogue and Leviticus 19, although the emphasis is on virtuous behaviour for its own sake rather than on religious motives for virtuous behaviour, an interesting shift back to the earliest motivations of wisdom sayings.

Although attributed to the Greek gnomic poet Phocylides, who lived in Miletus in Ionia in the mid-sixth century BC, these sentences are usually dated to the early first century AD, during the reigns of Augustus and Tiberias, possibly composed by a Jew in Alexandria, although the dating is uncertain. It consists of 230 hexameters, in dactyls, in the tradition of Greek and gnomic poetry. There are many sayings, linked often loosely by subject matter (cf. Ben Sira rather than Proverbs), which offer evidence of a rule of life for which the author wishes to argue. These musings are attributed to 'the most wise Phocylides'. Verses 3–8 are a selection from the Decalogue with the addition of a prohibition against homosexual practices (recalling Leviticus 18 and 20), and omission of any reference to the rejection of idolatry or of the sabbath. The final command – 'Honour God first and foremost and thereafter your parents' – alludes to the juxtaposition of God and parents in Leviticus

19. Verses 9–41 urge justice, recalling biblical laws about false witness, deposits and just measures and ending with a warning that 'If you judge wickedly, God will judge you thereafter'. Mercy toward the poor is then stressed, again with biblical overtones and some links with Ben Sira (Sir. 3:14; 4:10), although the maxims are less religiously motivated. Then come verses on the harm done by love of riches, vv. 42–7; cf. Sir. 8:2; 31:5), in which he questions the use of gold. There is some extolling of the traditional virtues of the sage – honesty, modesty, self-mastery and moderation – and expression of the idea that only God is truly wise and mighty (v. 54; possible overtones of Deut. 6:4; c.f. Sir. 1:8). He then speaks of avoiding envy and other vices (vv. 70–96). An emphasis on moderation is found in both Ben Sira and Hellenistic wisdom and has its roots in ancient Near Eastern thought and shows how difficult it is to trace the thought of an eclectic work such as this to any one tradition.

Another section treats death and the afterlife which includes the idea that human beings are the image of God (cf. Gen. 1—3) by their pneuma or spirit, their psyche or soul (vv. 105–6). There is evidence of such ideas in Hebrew thought (e.g. 1 Enoch and Jubilees) as well as Greek, although not in the wisdom literature. Along more Greek lines, however, the idea is expressed that the soul is immortal and even the body is destined to rise again. This is followed by a recitation of the uncertainties of life, urging the reader to adapt to circumstances. He praises wisdom using the language of personification: 'Better is a wise man than a strong one. Wisdom directs the course of lands and cities and ships' (vv. 130–1), especially prudence in speech (vv. 122–31). There is a strong emphasis on the human nature of wisdom rather than its God-given nature. The last three sections provide the closest parallels to the kind of practical wisdom taught by Ben Sira. He advises his readers to avoid vice and practise virtue and to have nothing to do with the evil practices of social outsiders or the unnatural practices of sorcerers (vv. 132–52). He praises work as a means of earning a living (vv. 153–74) – he uses the example of the ant and bee to encourage people to work (vv. 164–74; cf. Prov. 6:6–8 on ants) – and he provides advice for family life and relationships, including a list of prohibited sexual relations that recalls Leviticus 18 and 20 (vv. 175–227). The Sentences advocate marriage and contain warnings, like Ben Sira, against marrying a woman for her money, and about the importance of the chastity of daughters. There are warnings against homosexual practices, abortion and infanticide, all of which are trademarks of Jewish ethical teaching in the Hellenistic world in which homosexual practice was not forbidden.

The purpose for which the Sentences of Phocylides was written remains uncertain. Van der Horst (1988) argues that the author probably wrote this compendium of daily life for his fellow Jews to reassure them that Greek ethics essentially agreed with the Torah, that is to enable them to live as Jews in a Hellenistic environment and maintain an interest in Greek culture. It is likely to have been a school text, as was often the case with this kind of sayings text, both in relation to its wisdom precursors and its Greek counterparts. It is unlikely to be a propagandist Jewish text since it avoids mention of distinctively Jewish elements such as avoidance of adolatry, attending synagogue, circumcision, not marrying Gentiles and so on. However, J. J. Collins argues that the very use of the name Phocylides suggests that it was not just Jewish pupils that the author was trying to attract. Rather, he was desirous of promoting his understanding of the moral life. He sees the biblical overtones as incidental: 'He did not even inform his readers that these scriptures existed, any more than he lectured them on Plato or Stoicism. His purpose, the only purpose we can safely impute to him, was to impart to his readers, whether Jews or Gentiles, his understanding of the moral life' (1997b, p. 177). I wonder whether such a disinterested attitude to the Jewish background of thought indicated here can really be maintained, and I tend more towards van der Horst's conclusion

However, to return to the question whether this book is to be included as wisdom literature in the Israelite tradition, it can be seen to have been influenced particularly by Ben Sira. Furthermore, there are even overtones of the more universal wisdom of Proverbs, and yet there is seen to be such a broad drawing on various parts of the Bible by this stage – particularly the Torah – and considerable cultural interchange by this stage with Greek wisdom and philosophy that to speak of a distinctively Israelite wisdom tradition and even of a particularly Israelite wisdom influence as reflected in this work is a difficult task.

The Sentences of Sextus

We might also consider one or two later works (second century AD), notably the Sentences of Sextus, a work consisting of over four hundred proverbial-type maxims concerning the ideal life for Christians, more of a practical nature than containing any interest in the divine – you must shun gluttony, drunkenness, loquaciousness, marriage, the begetting of children and so on. At times the maxims are grouped around a common theme, but in most cases they are loosely strung together. There are overtones of proverbs in Proverbs and Ben Sira, for example Saying 155: 'Much talk does not escape sin' (cf. Proverbs 10:19: 'When words are many, transgression is not lacking'); and Saying 74: 'Let your reasoning (logos) precede your impulses' (cf. Sirach 37:16: 'Discussion is the beginning of every work, and counsel precedes every undertaking'). But this work is not specifically influenced by Jewish wisdom. It shows a number of similarities with the Greek gnomic tradition, in fact, and its interest in wisdom as a moral and religious category to describe humans rather than with wisdom as an attribute of God betrays its character as Hellenistic. As R. L. Wilken writes in his article 'Wisdom and Philosophy in Early Christianity', 'One does not have to turn to the books of Proverbs or Ecclesiasticus to obtain such advice as that offered in these sayings. Pithy and pointed sayings about fame or loquacity are as old as the human race' (1975, p. 149).

The Teachings of Silvanus

More links with Jewish wisdom are generally found in the Teachings of Silvanus (also second century AD) than in the Sentences of Sextus; yet again we encounter a Christianised form of Jewish wisdom which would be of very limited use in a definition of Israelite wisdom. Again styles and ideas are imitated and there is an interest in the figure of Wisdom that resembles most closely the Wisdom of Solomon. However, Silvanus is interested, unlike Sextus, in mystic-theosophical reflection – metaphysics rather than experience, probably influenced in large part by Hellenistic thought. As

W. R. Schoedel writes: 'Silvanus is ... an exhortation directed to Christians to receive the true light which shuts out the darkness and displays the uselessness of the things of this world' (1975, p. 194). He addresses the reader as 'my son'; cf, Proverbs 3:1f; Sir 12:12, and the opening exhortation is reminiscent of Proverbs 1:8, one of a number of calls of wisdom, an important theme in Silvanus. There are links too between the Wisdom of Solomon 7:25–6 and Silvanus 112.27—113.12 in the hymnic style. However, he stands in a fresh tradition that, if it draws on wisdom, is also drawing on much else and adapting it to new circumstances.

Philo of Alexandria

When we look at early interpreters we find the influence of wisdom on great thinkers such as Philo of Alexandria whose fondness for the wisdom literature was rivalled only by his devotion to the Torah, and thus who enjoyed using ideas and images from the wisdom tradition. A study of this work is of interest in seeing what types of themes from wisdom he thought were significant, but care has to be taken when studying Philo's use of Jewish wisdom because he alters what he appropriates and often mixes it with Greek concepts and images. One might also ask how self-consciously he actually differentiates wisdom ideas from a broader thought-world. This can be seen in the background to his Logos theory in which hokmâ is equated with Greek sophia and sophia with both Torah and Logos. He also explores ideas of Wisdom as an effluence or emanation of God's glory. Here it is interesting to see the influence of older traditions such as Proverbs 8 within a new context. The Jewish part of his thought here can be found in the idea of wisdom as a gift from God, present at creation and available to God as he shaped the world. That God bestows wisdom makes it kindred to God's revelation, his Torah, and so the two are synonymous. He takes the Hellenistic emphasis on wisdom as a human attribute and stresses the divine capacity of it. This use of the wisdom tradition by Philo does not affect our definition of the scope of wisdom literature, for by this time the definitive formulations have been made.

Concluding remarks

All these works show how wisdom retained an influence, although often in association with the ethics and law which can be seen to characterise Judaism. It is interesting that the ethical elements predominate in Judaism, while moral interest, but also cosmological interest, thrives in Christianity. Jews and Christians took what they wanted of the wisdom tradition to support what they were saying, as anyone would probably do if they were to write down their understanding of the world using wisdom images. Our understanding of wisdom is therefore enriched by this continuing tradition, although our basic definition of the extent of the wisdom literature remains unaffected. Wisdom influence can be found in these works, but not of a particularly Israelite kind.

11: WISDOM AT QUMRAN AND IN THE SAYINGS OF JESUS

> *By day and by night meditate on the mystery that is to come, and study it always. And then you will know truth and iniquity; wisdom and foolishness.* (4Q417 2 I 6–7, part of *Sapiential Work A*).

When we turn to the Qumran writings, a whole mass of scrolls discovered earlier this century by the shores of the Dead Sea and dating to the first century AD and earlier, we find among the sapiential works, many of them only recently published (see Elgvin et al., 1977, vol. 1), much the same problems of definition that have vexed our classification of wisdom so far. First, we find manuscripts of biblical wisdom books: there are fragments of the biblical books of Proverbs (4Q102, 103), Qoheleth (4Q109, 110) and Job (2Q15; 4Q99, 100, 101). There are also two Aramaic Targums of Job (4Q157, 11Q10). Two fragments of Sirach (2Q18) and also Sirach 51:13–19a are found in a Psalms scroll (11Q5). Beyond this we find extensive writings and sections of writings that have a claim to be included in the wisdom category. These are not primarily community documents and thus composed for the Qumran community, rather they are texts which in all probability predated the community itself. There are wisdom language and motifs in some of the sectarian texts, but these are not generally classified as wisdom works.

It is a majority view among scholars (A. S. van der Woude (1995); W. Lowndes Lipscomb and J. A. Sanders (1978)) that the Qumran community did not compose wisdom documents but that members of the community handed down writings of this kind and held them in esteem. This is not to regard them as merely library books, rather they represented a broader intellectual and religious heritage of which the community at Qumran were only a small part. There are scholars who would not agree; D. Dimant (1993), for example, attributes, on grounds of vocabulary, most of the sapiential texts discovered at Qumran to the Qumran community (with the exception of 4Q184, 4Q185, 4Q411 and 4Q412). J. J. Collins sums up the problem, 'Should they [the Dead Sea Scrolls] be regarded as products of the community, or communities, responsible for hiding them in the caves, or should they be viewed as part of the general heritage of Judaism around the turn of the era?' (*Jewish Wisdom in the Hellenistic Age*, 1997b, p. 113). The nature of the Qumran wisdom texts suggests the latter since they presuppose a wider society than just the isolated Qumran community.

Wisdom is becoming quite a broad concept by this period and it is clear that the community at Qumran participated in what was a common wisdom tradition. Furthermore, with the mixing of categories that began in the post-exilic period, it is becoming increasingly hard to distinguish genres of material anyway. While we find the language of wisdom in particular works which provides some criterion for aligning these texts, the main criterion for including texts as wisdom, as we found with Old Testament texts, is for their characteristics that recall mainstream wisdom literature. This means that we might want to characterise a text as wisdom only when it contains a number of wisdom elements, and otherwise it is better to speak only of wisdom influence.

Sapiential Work A

The most extensive wisdom material from Qumran is contained in Qumran Sapiential Work A which takes the form of a wisdom instruction along similar lines to those found in Proverbs 1—9. Six copies of this work were found at Qumran, suggesting that it was regarded as important there. It is set in a cosmological and eschatological framework but is mainly made up of a number of maxims placed randomly, as in Proverbs 22:17—24:22. Various topics are aired such as reward and punishment, dealings with different types of people, paying back loans, honouring parents, living in harmony with one's wife and children, and so on, which probably finds its context in some kind of instructional setting, with exhortations and advice to a 'poor' initiate forming a major feature: 'You are poor. Do not desire something beyond your share, and do not be confused by it, lest you displace your boundary' (4Q416 3. 8–9; quotations from Harrington, 1996a). There are warnings against selling oneself for money and against financial dealings with strangers. Part of the instruction (4Q415 2. 2. 1–9) is to a woman, the wife of the one under instruction. She is told to honour her father-in-law as her own father, to be faithful to her husband and their marriage and to be 'a subject of praise on the mouth of all men' – an unusual feature in wisdom literature. Another unusual feature of this instruction is that legal texts are cited as a starting point for wisdom instruction (e.g. Num. 30:6–15), which is used in the context of the husband's power to annul the vows and votive offerings of his wife (4Q416. 2. 4).

There are two emphases that depart from mainstream wisdom: one is that of seeing God as the source of all that is good, important and of value and on whom one can rely for a new identity; and the other is the eschatological element, notably the exhortation to meditate on 'the mystery that is to come', which is mentioned thirty times. What precisely this mystery is remains unclear, although Harrington (1996b) suggests that it is a reference to a body of teaching, written or oral, that has a fixed form. An identification with Torah is possible, but Harrington prefers the idea that it is an extra-biblical compendium, like the 'Book of Meditation' (1QSa 1. 6–8) or 'Maskil's Instruction' (1QS 3. 13–14, 26), or even the 'Book of Mysteries' (1Q27; 4Q299–301 – see below). J. J. Collins (1997a) argues from 4Q417 that, whilst the 'mystery that is to come' is repeatedly mentioned as an object of study, it also has an eschatological dimension and refers to the entire divine plan from creation to eschatological salvation and judgement.

In a recent article, Harrington (1997) compares Sirach and Sapiential Work A, arguing that they were roughly contemporary works. He argues that the emphasis in the work on financial dealings and on family life precludes an origin in the monastic setting of Qumran and that, like other wisdom texts, it was probably not composed especially for the community. Harrington looks at the forms contained in the two, and notes that numerical sayings, acrostics and, surprisingly, proverbs and the figure of wisdom are lacking in Sapiential Work A. He finds the content of each to have much in common on practical matters such as relations with one's wife and financial concerns, although Sapiential Work A presupposes the poverty of the one addressed, which is not true of Sirach or of biblical wisdom literature. He also notes the weaving in of Torah with wisdom concerns in both books, in the manner of some wisdom psalms (Pss. 1, 19, 119). However, he notes that it seems to have a much more apocalyptic character, with the emphasis on 'the mystery to come'. This kind of emphasis is conspicuously lacking in Sirach. There is furthermore a stronger emphasis in Sapiential Work A than in Sirach on God's activity in creation and human affairs, particularly in relation to the moral consequences of creation and divine election. The two works share a dualistic outlook in seeing two kinds of people, the righteous and the wicked, corresponding to good and evil in creation. However, Sapiential Work A puts more emphasis on God's activity in choosing the righteous and on the responsibility that the righteous therefore carry.

On the question of context Harrington finds both to belong to an instructional setting, both containing advice from elder to younger. Sapiential Work A may have belonged to a school such as that of Sirach. Harrington suggests that there are hints in 4Q417 2.1.1–17 that it is addressed to a future leader, possibly intended as a guide for training non-monastic leaders within a Jewish movement. Other alternatives are that it was a popular work at Qumran but not in any way associated with training there; or that it was composed especially for a non-monastic branch of the Qumran or Essene movement, even at their pre-Qumranic stage in the second century BC. Clearly, the context is uncertain, but the form and content reveal some interesting links with later Israelite wisdom literature and forge fresh links between wisdom and apocalyptic.

Psalms Scroll[a]

Other important sapiential documents are found on Psalms Scroll[a], including a description of David in 11Q5 27. 2–11 as 'wise and brilliant like the light of the sun; and a scribe, intelligent and perfect in all his ways before God and men'. This shows the uniting of roles of psalmist, wise man and prophet and of their common source of revelation; David is described as endowed with the spirit in the manner of a prophet, and yet divine revelation is also the source of his wisdom. We also find a Hymn to the Creator (11Q5 26.

9–15) that celebrates God's wisdom made known through his creative acts with reference to 'the knowledge of His heart . . . His wisdom . . . His understanding', recalling Psalm 135:7, Proverbs 8:22–31 and parts of Jeremiah.

In Psalm 154 (11Q5 18. 1–16, previously known only in Syriac) we find two stanzas concerning wisdom, the first emphasising the role of wisdom in praise of God. Wisdom is both the vehicle of revelation – a gift of God that makes known the glory of God – and the vehicle of human praise to God in recognition of his glory. The invitation is to all the community – 'the assembly of the pious' (line 10) – to join in praise to God. The language echoes Proverbs 8—9. The wisdom community is united in praise of God at meal times: 'When they eat in fullness, she is mentioned; and when they drink in community together, their meditation is on the Law of the Most High' (lines 11–12). This recalls the Qumran Community Rule (1QS 6) which demands that the community eat together and study the law continually. A link with the study of Torah is made here that recalls Sirach or the Torah psalms. Thus wisdom is manifested in meditation on the Law of the Lord (vv. 14–15). There is a positive appraisal of sacrifice and a clear relationship of wisdom to liturgical praise here.

Another sapiential element from the Psalms scroll is in fact part of Sirach – Sirach 51:13–19, 30 (11Q5 21. 11–17; 22. 1), an auto-biographical poem concerning the search for wisdom by the speaker accompanied by an invitation to others: 'When I was a young man before I travelled, I sought her. She came to me in her beauty, and unto the end I will search for her. As a blossom drops in the ripening of grapes, making glad the heart, so my foot walked on the straight path, for from my youth I knew her' (Sir. 51:13f, Cave 11 text). It refers to Wisdom as a nurse, tutor and mistress, passionately desired by the young man, and erotic imagery is used in the manner of the Song of Songs. There are overtones of Proverbs 5 and 7 and of Sirach 15. A version of this text appears in Sirach 51:13f. and 51:30b, thus suggesting its earlier provenance than the time of the community itself, although it may not be an original part of Ben Sira (see Chapter 8). It is written in the form of an acrostic and is a liturgical/cultic text (interesting evidence, along the lines of wisdom psalms, for a closer link between wisdom and cult).

Folly and Wisdom in 4Q184–5

Other sapiential texts include 4Q184 1, known as 'The Wiles of the Wicked Woman' (R. D. Moore, 1979–81), containing a description of Lady Folly and reminiscent of and possibly dependent on Proverbs 2, 5, 7 and 9. It describes the fate of those seduced by Lady Folly and introduces an element of everlasting damnation absent from the Proverbs version:

> Her beds are couches of corruption... depths of the pit, her lodgings are beds of darkness. In the deep of night are her tents; in the foundations of gloom she sets up her dwelling, and she inhabits the tents of silence. Amidst everlasting fire is her inheritance, not among all those who shine brightly. (lines 5–7)

The description of Lady Folly as 'the beginning of all the ways of iniquity' (line 8) is a play on the description of her counterpart Lady Wisdom in Proverbs 8:22. Furthermore, her victims are not just the simple and foolish as in Proverbs but the righteous themselves. It has been suggested that Lady Folly is a symbol for the opponents of the Qumran community, but it seems more likely to refer to those within the community who might be given to such temptations as represented by this figure. In the context of a sectarian group, the two ways, one of righteousness and the other of wickedness, have particular resonances for those who consider themselves the righteous. However, there is no actual reference to the Qumran community in 4Q184, which suggests that it did not originate there.

4Q185 1–2 is part of a wisdom instruction which contains calls to 'you simple', 'my sons', 'sons of men' and 'my people' to pay attention and contains commands, prohibitions and warnings of judgement by angels: 'And who can endure to stand before His angels? For with a flaming fire they will judge... of His spirits' (1. 8–9). There are emphases on the wrath of God and the fragility of humankind (cf. Job 14:1; Isa. 40:6–8; Pss. 90:5–6; 103:15–16). There is a link with the past in the recalling of past deeds such as the Exodus in the manner of Psalm 78 and Ben Sira, and we find the theme of the two ways. There is also a 'Happy is . . .' beatitudes section outlining wisdom as a gift of God and her benefits to those who seek her and remain faithful to her: 'Happy is the man to whom she has been given' (2. 8); 'Seek her and find her and hold fast to her and get her as an inheritance. With her is length of days and fatness of bone and joy of heart' (2. 12). There is a sense in this of wisdom being available to all, and not simply to be equated with the law, although we also find the idea that God chooses to give wisdom to some – 'Israel' is mentioned in 2. 10 – and not to 'the wicked' (2. 9).

Other sapiential texts

There are many other fragments that have a claim to be included in the wisdom corpus. There are some further instructions, notably 4Q424 and 4Q525. 4Q424 warns the young against crooked and incompetent people: 'A man devious in speech – do not trust him to pronounce judgment in your favour' (1. 8). Following the style of admonition found in Proverbs – that of advice and instruction – the piece focuses on a number of negative social phenomena, offering advice to the addressee not to do these things. The emphasis then shifts towards positive descriptions of more reliable and upstanding figures who are versed in the ways of wisdom in fragment 3. 7b–11, at what is probably the climax to the document (see Brin, 1977): 'An upright man will delight in justice. A man of truth will rejoice in a proverb' (3. 8).

4Q525 is a series of fragments, some of which contain wisdom instruction and others of which contain beatitudes. In the wisdom instructions there are sections on the rewards of pursuing wisdom, including wise choice of words, and contrasts are drawn between the rewards of righteousness and the punishment of wickedness. In the beatitudes, Wisdom and the Law of Moses are identified in a way that recalls Sirach 24. These are often likened to the beatitudes in the Gospels. The message in the beatitudes here is that the law of God is to be obeyed as the source of all life and blessing, e.g. 'Happy is the man [who] has attained wisdom, and walks by the Law of the Most High' (2. ii. 3–4).

There are some texts which are more eschatological in their

focus (e.g. the Book of Mysteries 1Q27 and 4Q299–301). The Book of Mysteries also concerns itself with 'the mystery that is to come' and envisages a time when wickedness is removed and righteousness will reign for ever: 'And all who cling to the mysteries of wonder will be no more, and knowledge will fill the world, and folly will be there no more' (1Q27 1. 6–7). The foolish are those who do not consider the former things and who cannot discern between good and evil because they do not know 'the mystery that is to come'. Access to a vision which imparts wisdom is granted to the sect alone, and this departs radically from the universalism of mainstream wisdom literature.

There are texts which emphasise the two ways of righteous-ness and wicked people, such as 4Q420–421, which highlights the characteristics of a wise and righteous person: 'He will not speak before he understands, and with patience he will give a reply' (1. ii. 2–3). There are also hymns such as 4Q413, the 'hymn of knowledge', which concerns itself with the way of wisdom, with God's plan for humankind and with the rewards of pursuing righteousness over folly: '[Knowledge] and wisdom I will teach you, and get under-standing in the ways of humankind and in the deeds of the children of humanity' (line 1). There are also some esoteric sectarian works such as 4Q298 1, the '[Wo]rd of a *maskil* that he spoke to all the sons of dawn' (1–2 i. 1), which is written in a cryptic script and is a manual of instruction. Here we are in the realm of sectarian writings and we can begin to look into sectarian writings for wisdom influ-ence: e.g. Damascus Document 2, 'God loves knowledge, Wisdom and understanding He has set before Him, and prudence and knowl-edge serve Him' (ii 2–3), and the 'Instruction on the Two Spirits' in the Community Rule which includes sapiential elements. These are not to be included as wisdom texts from Qumran; rather, they are Qumran sectarian texts that show some wisdom influence. The lines between the two categories can scarcely be drawn, because once wisdom becomes a part of the language and daily parlance of the sect, then the inclusion of its ideas and imagery would be more surprising for its absence than its presence. Features of the nature of wisdom in sectarian documents have been explored by scholars (e.g. Newsom, 1990), and recently R. C. van Leeuwen (1997) has argued for a particular kind of scribal wisdom, interested in using scripture as expressing its vision of reality, as a keynote of wisdom in the sectarian texts.

Criteria for inclusion as wisdom texts

The only real criteria we can use to decide whether to include works under the wisdom umbrella are those that we have already set up, so that on the level of form we find instructions, poems and hymns that resemble forms found in Proverbs and Sirach in particular. We also find 'happy are . . .' sayings or beatitudes. On the level of content, familiar topics emerge such as concern with money, social relations, family. We also find the figure of Wisdom featuring prominently, accompanied by an interest in creation and a link up between wisdom and law. Thus both the anthropological and the cosmological sides of wisdom are represented in this literature as elsewhere, with practical admonitions pertaining to conduct in life, represented on the one hand, and wisdom as the key to understanding the cosmos and world order represented on the other. Fresh developments seem to include the idea of wisdom as a gift of God and the emphasis on wisdom both as a reason for praise and as the enabler of it, and on future mysteries in the manner of apocalyptic.

We find a surprisingly broad context that does not seem to have been affected by sectarianism – and yet we can also find wisdom elements in sectarian texts which suggest that more universal texts were read in a sectarian manner (e.g. wisdom influence on the Community Rule (1QS and 1QSa) and thanksgiving hymns (e.g. 1QH); see Stuckenbruck, 1999). Thus in the Qumran material we find a microcosm of the wisdom literature that we have identified. Sapiential Work A is a mainstream wisdom work, while other works really belong to another genre, but have close similarities also to wisdom – such as parts of the Psalm Scroll[a]. Certain works that are on the edges of the wisdom group such as the Book of Mysteries. Wisdom at Qumran is a natural successor of Sirach, in particular in its emphasis on divine wisdom, on the link between wisdom and Torah, on praise of God and on its ethical quest. However, it contains elements of the liturgical, the esoteric and the eschatological that go beyond the confines of the wisdom genre as found in the later wisdom books.

Wisdom, mantic wisdom and apocalyptic

The nature of wisdom at Qumran links up with a wider debate about the origins of apocalyptic literature. As mentioned in Chapter 6, prophecy has traditionally been seen as the forerunner of apocalyptic, although this was countered by von Rad ([1958–61] 1962b) who saw it as having its roots in wisdom. My conclusion above was that both prophecy and wisdom contributed to apocalyptic, although it was a later kind of mantic wisdom that had more influence than mainstream wisdom ideas. This links up with Qumran in the apocalyptic emphasis in many of the wisdom texts that we have been considering. This apocalyptic emphasis has itself come in under the influence of works such as Daniel and Enoch that were popular among the writings of the sect, and so we find wisdom itself changing under fresh influences. The link between mantic wisdom and apocalyptic leads J. C. VanderKam to look further at divinatory texts in the Qumran writings. He argues: 'There was great interest in astronomical data at Qumran, but few of the texts explicitly turn them to divinatory uses . . . the focus of mantic activity was the interpretation of what the group considered authoritative scripture' (1997, pp. 352–3).

Wisdom in the sayings of Jesus

> 'Where did this man get this wisdom and these deeds of power?'
> (Matthew 13:54)

There is little doubt that Jesus said many wise things. One of his chief roles was as a teacher; and he gave, both to his disciples and to larger groups, instruction in how to live their lives in a meaningful way in the light of the revelation that he came to bring. However, there is a difference, as we have seen, between being wise in a general sense and having anything to do with the wisdom tradition, and it is this latter category that I wish to explore here.

Jesus' use of wisdom genres

The question we face regarding Jesus and the wisdom tradition is whether Jesus used wisdom genres in his speech, and whether what he had to say in his teaching was the same kind of reflection on human relationships as we find in the proverbs. L. G. Perdue (1986) has done a study of the various different types of proverb in the book of Proverbs and their relationship to the sayings of Jesus in the Gospels. He finds examples of short, pithy one-line proverbs, such as 'No one can serve two masters' (Matt. 6:24; Luke 16:13). He finds examples of synonymous proverbs, in which two related sentiments are put alongside, e.g. Matthew 10:24 (Luke 6:40a; John 13:16; 15:20; cf. Prov. 24:5), 'A disciple is not above his teacher, nor a slave above his master'; antithetical proverbs which involve a contrast, e.g. Matthew 8:20 (Luke 9:58; c.f. Prov. 10:31), 'Foxes have holes, and birds of the air have nests; but the Son of Man has nowhere to lay his head'; and synthetical proverbs in which the two halves of the verse agree, e.g. Luke 6:38 (Matt. 7:2; cf. Prov. 15:31), 'The measure you give, will be the measure you get back.' He finds three types of comparative proverb, the first which uses 'like' or 'as', e.g. Matthew 13:52, 'And he said to them, "Therefore every scribe who has been trained for the kingdom of heaven is like the master of a household who brings out of his treasure what is new and what is old"' (c.f. Prov. 26:11); a second type that uses the idea of less and more, e.g. Luke 16:10, 'Whoever is faithful in a very little is faithful also in much; and whoever is dishonest in a very little is dishonest also in much' (cf. Prov. 15:11); and a third comparative type of 'better' saying, e.g. Mark 10:25 (Matt. 19:24; Luke 18:25), 'It is easier for a camel to go through the eye of a needle than for someone who is rich to enter the kingdom of God' (cf. Prov. 16:8). There are a few other wisdom types that he considers, such as numerical sayings and rhetorical questions of which there are a few parallels in the gospel tradition. We may also consider thematic parallels and note that many of the wise sayings of Jesus are not on the same subjects as proverbial wisdom – many major themes such as proverbs about hard work and warnings about loose women are totally absent from Jesus' words (Witherington III, 1994). Rather, he is concerned with ethical behaviour but always with the coming kingdom in mind. We may also look at interesting, but not exact, parallels between maxims and beatitudes in Ben Sira and the maxims and beatitudes of Jesus.

A study of the parallels provides conclusive evidence for a strong connection between Jesus and the wisdom tradition, at least on a literary level. It is significant that many of the parallels are from the tradition shared by Matthew and Luke only and are probably therefore from the shared sayings source 'Q'. Some were shared by Mark, which, as the earliest Gospel, perhaps increases their claim to historicity. Fewer examples are to be found in the Matthean and Lukan sources on their own. Thus the majority of the wisdom-type sayings of Jesus are common-source material from either Mark or more often from Q. This raises a further question for us: in drawing these parallels between Jesus and wisdom should we regard Jesus himself as a kind of wise teacher standing in a common wisdom tradition, or is this in fact a picture enhanced by the incorporation of this separate sayings source, Q, which may nevertheless contain an authentic record of his words, into the presentation of his ministry by the gospel writers? Maybe it was Q that contained all this wisdom in the interests of presenting Jesus as a wise man, to shift the focus away from his being an apocalyptic visionary whose predictions about the end had not yet come. We could back up this assertion with a glimpse at the Epistle of James, a letter containing a strong wisdom element in which, however, futuristic, apocalyptic elements come under the wisdom umbrella so that the book retains a practical reality about the present and distances the emphasis on the end time.

Character of Jesus' sayings

As well as using traditional wisdom forms, Jesus also employs a personal, instructive technique. He speaks of his own person and significance using wisdom formulations, e.g. Mark 8:35 (c.f. Matt. 10:39; Luke 17:37 and John 12:25): 'For whoever would save his life will lose it; and whoever loses his life for my sake and the gospel's will save it.' This has the character of an antithetical saying, but is formulated in a new way that speaks of eternal life, and in a veiled way of his eschatological significance. Jesus also speaks by use of this kind of wisdom saying about the coming of the kingdom, e.g. Luke 6:20b: 'Blessed are you who are poor, for yours is the kingdom of God' – a 'blessed are' saying shaped with an eschatological perspective that is an innovation in the wisdom tradition before Qumran. Perdue (1986) lists admonitions (e.g. Luke 9:60), 'better than' sayings (e.g. Mark 9:43, c.f. Matt. 5:30; 18:8), numerical sayings (e.g. Matt. 19:12) and instruction (e.g. Matt. 9:42–50) that are all shaped by Jesus into a fresh framework of proclamation of the kingdom or musing on questions of eternal life or eternal damnation. Jesus is here giving wisdom sayings a new context in the light of the events of the kingdom that are about to break in on the present.

Therefore, at first sight, the links between Jesus and wisdom appear to be considerable. Jesus is presented in the Gospels as a kind of wisdom teacher standing in a common wisdom tradition. However, we need to remember two points. The first is that a number of these maxims belong to the Q tradition shared by Matthew and Luke which has been considered to be a separate sayings source with a particular wisdom interest. We may have to exercise caution therefore in saying that this wisdom emphasis came straight from Jesus himself, although many of the sayings may have done. Second, when we analyse the material closely, while Jesus uses many proverb types, he also expresses new and radical ideas about the in-breaking of the kingdom and the significance of his own self that go beyond traditional proverbial ideas. Another example might be Mark 2:27–8: 'And he said to them, "The sabbath was made for humankind, and not humankind for the sabbath; so the Son of Man is lord even of the sabbath." ' Here a general saying is extended into a specific comment about who Jesus is. This individual character of Jesus' sayings stands out: he is not commenting on common human experience here; rather, his is the individual voice speaking of the breaking-in of the kingdom. Jesus asserts a counter order to the status quo, a better state of affairs that can come to pass beyond the confines of traditional wisdom.

Thus although there appears to be a close relationship between the kind of general maxims found in wisdom and those in the Gospels, we need to be cautious of limiting the sayings of Jesus by the comparison. He goes a step further than traditional proverbial wisdom in speaking of God's kingdom that will change the traditional

modes of thinking once and for all. However, he does not ignore
more traditional wisdom and we can certainly find evidence of its
genres in the sayings attributed to him, even though we cannot be
sure to what extent it goes back to Jesus himself. Since Q is regarded
as a very early source along with Mark it is likely that the historical
Jesus was engaged in the transmission of wisdom in both a traditional
and an untraditional sense. It may be that his sayings in the Q source
were given a more formal wisdom structure by those who compiled
it, but it is likely that much of it goes back to Jesus himself.

We would no doubt fall short of classifying Jesus as a professional wise man. Perhaps rather we should see him as a kind of
wise radical who used what he wanted of the traditional ideas, so
that his words resonated with elements of what people already knew
and understood, but who challenged the tradition with new ideas and
so shaped old wisdom into a new context. Many of the wisdom
writers, such as the author of Ecclesiastes and Ben Sira, were clearly
highly educated men, and there are questions whether wise men
had connections with royal courts. Clearly, Jesus was not in this
category. He was educated but probably not in a highly formalised
way. He probably knew a good deal of folk-wisdom and of course he
knew his Bible, the Old Testament, and the wisdom contained in it,
but he also had a new message of his own to convey in language
that people could understand. There may have been temple schools
or synagogues in this later period in which Jesus may have been
educated at some point – there is the story of him listening and
asking questions in the temple at Jerusalem (Luke 2:46) – but his
precise educational context is unknown. Despite not being in an
official wise role, as with many who have a profound influence on
human thought his wisdom in many ways surpassed that of the
professionals.

Parables

A question has been raised regarding Jesus' technique of
telling parables and the wisdom tradition. It is interesting that this
is one of the major teaching methods Jesus used (see T. W. Manson
(1957) for a discussion of the forms used by Jesus in his teaching),
but actually it is not common in the wisdom tradition. There is

autobiographical narrative as we have noted, and a possible parable about a poor wise man delivering a city by his wisdom in Ecclesiastes 9:14–15. We also have Jotham's fable and analogies in Isaiah 5 and in Ezekiel. Parables are comparisons in the form of a story or extended similes. They are universal illustrations in one sense but they often have a historical character in having a particular context in time and place. The fact that the parable is not a standard wisdom form perhaps points to the conclusion that in his criticism of the status quo Jesus developed distinctive methods of teaching of his own. As B. B. Scott writes: 'The construct of the voice of Jesus' aphorisms or parables embodies a distinctive, individual voice whose patterns, accents, styles, themes, and even ideology are recognizable. This is to be distinguished from other proverbs and parables whose voice, being "anonymous" is the projection of common wisdom' (1990, p. 407).

Concluding remarks

Much of Jesus' own 'wisdom' is that of one who wishes to build upon much of the received wisdom and add fresh forms and ideas of his own to express his own vision of the coming kingdom. He challenged the old ways of thinking, going beyond simply the reiteration of maxims and proverbs for others and went into the realms of eschatology to proclaim the coming of God's kingdom. In this sense his words cross the boundary between wisdom and apocalyptic and we need not look far to find similarities with the musings of the Qumran writers on 'the mystery that is to come'.

12: WISDOM'S PLACE, CONTRIBUTION AND LEGACY

To get wisdom is to love oneself; to keep understanding is to prosper. (Prov. 19:8)

In this book I have attempted both to focus on the mainstream wisdom literature of the Old Testament and Apocrypha and to show how widespread the influence of wisdom both within the Old Testament and outside it has been. I have looked both at wisdom's origins in the ancient Near East and at its widening influence on later material in the Jewish and Greek world, considering Qumran and the sayings of Jesus in particular.

I have been concerned with problems of definition in an attempt to limit the discussion, on the one hand, and, using Proverbs as a starting point, to provide a set of criteria by which to evaluate any wisdom book. This has led to the finding that Job, generally considered a mainstream wisdom book, and many of the wisdom psalms, are on the edges of a close definition. In this finding lies the reason for attempting to chart the extent of a wider wisdom influence in the Old Testament and beyond. Wisdom is thus shown to be a much greater and less defined phenomenon in these wider terms and yet with an identifiable presence in a large number of works. In fact, there is virtually no part of the Old Testament canon that is entirely free from wisdom influence, given that it extends into narrative, law, psalmody and prophecy, and goes on to have an influence on apocalyptic. Nor does wisdom's influence cease as the canon closes. Its influence goes on to be far-reaching as it comes into contact with fresh cultures, notably with the Greek world and with Christianity.

I have argued throughout that wisdom influence is not to be regarded as late scribal editing of texts, but rather that the influence was a formative one, indicating that wisdom genres were part of everyday speech and a well-known means of self-expression, especially, on a literary level, among the more educated. It is likely that, in the shaping of wisdom and other works as literary texts, the educated may have introduced elements of wisdom from their own more intellectual thought-world. However, it is my view that the wisdom enterprise cannot be restricted to scribal circles; rather, that its antiquity and widespread nature could well have led to its being a formative influence upon texts, even upon the oral formulations of texts, as they became known and gradually written down. I have shown, in particular in relation to non-wisdom texts influenced by the genre, how this process may have occurred. Thus wisdom influence is found in a wide range of material – in psalms, prophets, apocalyptic, pentateuchal and narrative texts – and is revealed as a particular way of looking at the world and at humanity's place in it.

Place

Wisdom's place has always been somewhat ambivalent. It is often regarded by scholars as having been on the margins of the thought-world of the Old Testament until, in the apocryphal wisdom books of Sirach and the Wisdom of Solomon, it found a central place in its association with the law, with prayer and prophecy, and with the saving history. As J. Bright wrote: 'Some parts of the Old Testament are far less clearly expressive of Israel's distinctive understanding of reality than others, some parts (and one thinks of such a book as Proverbs) seem to be only peripherally related to it, while others (for example Ecclesiastes) even question its essential features' (1967, p. 136). It has also been downgraded by scholars because of such presuppositions and has had a less important role in the shaping of Old Testament theologies than is fair to it. A recent Old Testament theology by H. D. Preuss ([1991] 1995–6), for example, makes little of the role of wisdom literature. The central problem with this perspective is the presupposition that, in fact, it is the salvation history that is at the centre of concern in the Old Testament. Once wisdom is seen as an alternative world-view of stature, importance and widespread influence, with a central theological role, then that perspective starts to change.

I have tried to argue for the distinctiveness of wisdom as a separate tradition, with wider roots in ancient Near Eastern thought, but nevertheless with its own special place within the life of Israel too. Its very different starting point gives it a distinctiveness that makes it easily identifiable, and its forms too are sufficiently defined so that it does not get lost in a mass of other genres. Thus when wisdom forms, content and context are found together in large measure we are in the realm of wisdom literature, but when they are found sporadically we should more readily speak of wisdom influence on texts. This extended influence indicates its formative influence and importance in the shaping of all kinds of ideas in all kinds of circumstances. We have seen how wisdom influence on the Psalter and on the prophets in shaping expressions about the natural world and in maxims about appropriate behaviour is particularly marked. The influence is not solely one-way: cultic forms have entered the wisdom corpus, and a tendency towards the prophetic is found, particularly in the later wisdom material, and also in Proverbs in the description of the figure of wisdom (notably in Proverbs 1:20–33). This suggests that wisdom is not to be marginalised; rather, its significant and lasting place should be affirmed afresh.

Wisdom is a form of expression that cuts across more historical presentations of the faith. In that sense it has close links with worship in the immediacy with which it directs questions at God. The lamenting of Job has much in common with psalms of lament as well as with certain wisdom psalms; the pessimism of Ecclesiastes likewise with certain wisdom psalms, and even the pragmatism of Proverbs has its place in cultic life. This tendency to link up with the worshipping life of Israel becomes more overt in the later wisdom books and suggests that teaching, learning and prayerfulness are not entirely divorced concepts.

Contribution

Wisdom begins with experience, human experience of the world and of God as creator and sustainer of that world. Wisdom has at once a practical dimension and a more profound theological aspect. It represents the cumulative experience of many generations, distilled into pithy, memorable sayings for easy remembering. It offers advice, exhortation and warning on everyday matters. And yet its contribution is more profound theologically than just this practical aspect; it is the meeting of the two aspects that gives wisdom its distinctiveness.

We saw in our discussion of Proverbs how the figure of wisdom in Proverbs 8 allowed a profundity to enter the debate on a theological level that was lacking in the maxim-making, although God was not absent from that activity either. This was seen to be taken up in the hymns to wisdom in Job, Sirach and the Wisdom of Solomon. I have argued that wisdom was never a secular enterprise but that it was a more theological quest, with an equal emphasis on the divine as on the human. I have argued that in this figure of wisdom the tension can best be seen between the human quest for understanding and the divine revelation to humanity. The figure of wisdom in Proverbs offers the fear of God and knowledge of God as a gift (Prov. 2:5–8). Wisdom offers to lead a person on the right way if only the person will trust in her rather than in their own skill. In this is contained the offer of salvation – this is the path to life rather than the path to death. Wisdom is the essence of what human beings need for a meaningful life, and as the form in which Yahweh makes himself present and in which he wishes to be sought by humankind: 'The Lord, by wisdom founded the earth; by understanding he established the heavens' (Prov. 3:19). Wisdom is a constructive principle by which Yahweh allowed himself to be guided in the construction of the world. It represents order, as reflected both in creation and the natural world and in the relationship of human beings and society. Wisdom is also a personal call: it can be acquired, sought and 'got', and yet it can also be missed or forsaken. Wisdom on her side preserves the person who trusts in her, and makes a person well-pleasing in the sight of Yahweh. In Proverbs 8 wisdom is described as in existence before all God's work of creation, the first-born of creatures (Prov. 8:22) and yet reaching out to human beings to keep her ways.

It is when this relationship seems to be out of balance that we find ourselves entering the lamenting and questioning realm of Job, Ecclesiastes and the wisdom psalms. There is a sense of God as creator whose ways are above human comprehension. Wisdom here touches the limits. The poem on wisdom in Job 28 makes this point, that the depths of God's wisdom far exceed human attempts to uncover it. Humans may have great technical ability to search deep in the bowels of the earth, using sophisticated mining techniques, but the nature of the quest is essentially different. Ultimately, despite human control over the natural world, there are limits to human knowledge, and these are gaps that can never be filled. There will always be areas of knowledge that are impenetrable and this is the realm of God. This is God's wisdom which is in the world and represents the rational purpose through which the universe was created, but which is ultimately inaccessible to human comprehension. This is contrasted at the end of Job 28 with the kind of wisdom that is within human grasp, a practical wisdom or mode of living. The same kind of message is found in God's speeches in Job and in the poem on time in Ecclesiastes. There is particular concern in Job with the question of just retribution, and this is found also in the psalms and in the later wisdom books.

The interrelationship of the human and divine has been described by L. G. Perdue as a dialectic between anthropology and cosmology. He writes: 'The dialectic of anthropology and cosmology is far more inclusive of the variety of expression that characterises the complexity of creation thought in wisdom literature' (1991, p. 20). This two-pronged tradition of cosmology and anthropology clearly comes together in Proverbs, with a weighting towards the human quest for wisdom in its older sections but with the dialectic apparent in Proverbs 1—9, especially in Proverbs 8. This was followed in the early post-exilic period by the composition of Job and Ecclesiastes, in part as a critique of the picture found in Proverbs. Job can be seen as representing the tension between the two prongs of the tradition, the dialogue between Job and the friends representing the limits of the more humanistic debate, and the relationship between Job and God representing the clash of the anthropocentric with the cosmological. Ecclesiastes too illustrates both sides of the tradition – a use of proverbial wisdom, be it often to contradict, and yet an appeal to the cosmological God and his unpredictability in poems such as 3:1–11.

This tension can also be evidenced in the hymns to wisdom in Proverbs 8:22f, Job 28 and Sirach 24 and the Wisdom of Solomon 7:22—8:2 in their movement between God's creative activity and human perception. The pattern of these poems shows a move from God to humanity and back again to the human need to respond to God for the acquisition of life (but often human folly in not doing so). We can also find this pattern in the Logos hymn in John 1 in which we find the action of God initiating the revelation that is Jesus, but the human response too in receiving him. It is God who is the initiator of life, but it is human beings to whom that life is offered. At the climax of John's prologue in verses 10–13 is the response of humans to the light and the offer of life for those who receive him. In Genesis 1, God makes humans the climax of his creation and fashions them in his own image. God is striving for a relationship with human beings and so, in John, the Word became flesh to offer them life. There is a deliberate structuring of the pattern of all these wisdom poems to show that the human side is inextricably bound up with the cosmic and that the two meet. It is in this conundrum that the heart of the wisdom enterprise lies.

In maintaining a two-sided wisdom tradition, I am arguing against those who perceive wisdom in a straight line of development from a more basic, anthropocentric concept to a more developed theological one. I have argued elsewhere (Dell, 1995) that developments tend to take place at different times and that we have been too tied to such concerns. However, this conclusion does affect other conclusions about context. In seeing wisdom in this more theological way, it makes more anthropocentric theories that confine wisdom to court and school less attractive, and broader theories of family education, widespread maxim-making and a link-up with the worshipping life of Israel more so. We have seen how the Joseph and Succession Narratives were largely included by scholars as wisdom literature on the basis of the presupposition of a context allowing court and administration to be at the forefront of concern (cf. the figure of Daniel also). It is clear that it would not be right to confine the production of wisdom to one or two contexts. It has early origins in the oral world, possibly an influence from a wider thought-world. Its educational role is apparent, although it was broader than just the preserve of the educated. Yet there were specialists, those who had the leisure for learning and were gifted in writing, who may have been responsible both for wisdom texts and for the shaping of other texts. And yet, the wisdom phenomenon is not a scribal one either; it is a thought-world distinct and separate, but infiltrating life at all levels. It is thus an ambiguous and multifarious concept which is difficult to pin down. It did enter the realm of the theological at various points – perhaps more overtly later on in Job and Ecclesiastes, but I hold that it never perceived the world without God and that the interrelationship between the human and the divine was there from the start.

Legacy

Among some scholars there is opening up a recognition of a world-view to be found in wisdom that was not as historically bound as other parts of the Old Testament. This world-view has the creative acts of God as its central focus. For example, C. Westermann has made a distinction between the saving acts of God in history and blessing from God as a constant action beyond the temporal realm. He relates wisdom closely to this latter kind of blessing and writes: 'The word that is formed by wisdom, experience, and maturity is the fruit of blessing' ([1968] 1978, p. 38). He relates Job also to 'blessing', seeing it as a tale of the bestowal and witholding of blessing and he finds connections between creation and blessing in the God speeches. He finds an important role for blessing in worship too. He describes blessing from God as 'the power that establishes and furthers life, growth and prosperity, and protects from harm and danger' (1978, p. 41). Along similar lines, B. Gemser (1975) speaks of a horizontal and a vertical revelation existing alongside one another and in tension. J. Lévêque (1974) likewise speaks of a contrapuntal relationship between two main themes of wisdom: concern for a structuring of the created and the existence of humanity on the one hand, and the rest of the Old Testament on the other.

It is a strong possibility in my view that, 'a cosmology from wisdom which saw God in all things as creator . . . existed alongside and in tension with a more maxim-based wisdom, which nevertheless uses images from the created world to illuminate human behaviour . . . started from human experience and saw God at its limits. However, neither is ever conceived of apart from God' (Dell, 1997). This kind of faith represented a profound interaction with the natural world, shared by Israel to a certain extent with its neighbours. As H. H. Schmid wrote: 'The controlling background of Old Testament thought and faith is the view of a comprehensive world order and, hence, a creation faith in the broad sense of the word – a creation faith that Israel in many respects shared with her environment' (1984, pp. 110–11). This in turn existed alongside more historical presentations of Israel's faith and at times came into close contact, such as in the later wisdom books of Sirach and the Wisdom of Solomon.

Wisdom's legacy then is to have given to the Israelites an alternative world-view. As J. L. Crenshaw writes:

> The sages offered an alternative mode of interpreting reality to the Yahwistic one in which God was actively involved in guiding history toward a worthy goal . . . In their view, revelation took place during the creative act, and when human capacity to discover this hidden mystery seemed inadequate, God continued to make known his will through personified wisdom. (1982, pp. 208–9).

The origins of this alternative world-view may be found in the ancient Near Eastern world, but its roots in Israelite thought are also powerful. It is to be seen as a widespread and influential phenomenon, less distinctively Israelite than historical and covenantal categories, but part of the thought-world of which Israel was a part. The Israelite appropriation of wisdom was something distinctive – they did not simply borrow unthinkingly, and the contexts in which wisdom was practised were not identical. As a particular understanding of reality its theology permeated all corners of Israelite thought, and hence wisdom influence is strong both within the Old Testament and outside it.

BIBLIOGRAPHY

Alonso–Schokel, L. (1975) 'Sapiential and Covenant Themes in Genesis 2—3', in *Studies in Ancient Israelite Wisdom*, ed. J. L. Crenshaw, New York: KTAV, pp. 468–80.

Alster, B. (1974) *Studies in Sumerian Proverbs*, Copenhagen: Akademisk Forlag.

Barton, J. (1979) 'Natural Law and Poetic Justice in the Old Testament', *JTS* NS 30, pp. 1–14.

Barton, J. (1980) *Amos' Oracles to the Nations*, SOTS Monograph Series 6, Cambridge: Cambridge University Press.

Batten, L. W. (1933) 'The Epilogue to the Book of Job', *Anglican Theological Review* 15, pp. 125–8.

Baumgartner, W. (1914) 'Der literarischen Gattungen in der Weisheit des Jesus Sirach', *ZAW* 34, pp. 161–98.

Beauchamp, P. (1975) 'Épouser la Sagesse – on n'épouse qu'elle?' in *La Sagesse de l'ancien Testament*, ed. M. Gilbert, Louvain: Gembloux, pp. 347–69.

Besserman, L. L. (1979) *The Legend of Job in the Middle Ages*, Cambridge MA: Harvard University Press.

Boston, J. R. (1968) 'Wisdom Influence upon the Song of Moses', *JBL* 87, pp. 198–202.

Braun, R. (1973) *Kohelet und die frühhellenistiche Popularphilosophie*, BZAW 130, Berlin: Walter de Gruyter.

Brenner, A. (1989) 'Job, the Pious? The Characterization of Job in the Narrative Framework of the Book', *JSOT* 43, pp. 37–52.

Bright, J. (1967) *The Authority of the Old Testament*, London: SCM Press.

Brin, G. (1997) 'Wisdom Issues in Qumran. The Types and Status of the Figures in 4Q424 and the Phrases of Rationale in the Document', *DSD* 4/3, pp. 297–311.

Brueggemann, W. (1972) *In Man We Trust*, Atlanta: John Knox Press.

Brueggemann, W. (1991) 'Bounded by Obedience and Praise: The Psalms as Canon', *JSOT* 50, pp. 63–92.

Bryce, G. E. (1979) *A Legacy of Wisdom. The Egyptian Contribution to the Wisdom of Israel*, Lewisburg: Bucknell University Press.

Camp, C. V. (1985) *Wisdom and the Feminine in the Book of Proverbs*, Sheffield: Almond Press.

Charlesworth, J. H. (1983) *The Old Testament Pseudepigrapha, Volume 1: Apocalyptic Literature and Testaments*, London: Darton, Longman and Todd.

Childs, B. S. (1965) 'The Birth of Moses', *JBL* 84, pp. 109–22.

Christianson, E. (1998) *A Time to Tell: Narrative Strategies in Ecclesiastes*, JSOTS 280, Sheffield: Sheffield Academic Press.

Clements, R. E. (1992) *Wisdom in Theology*, Carlisle: Paternoster Press; Grand Rapids MI: Eerdmans.

Clines, D. J. A. (1989) *Job 1—20*, Word Biblical Commentary 17, Dallas, TX: Word Books.

Coats, G. W. (1973) 'The Joseph Story and Ancient Wisdom: A Reappraisal', *CBQ* 25, pp. 285–97.

Collins, J. J. (1997a) 'Wisdom Reconsidered, in Light of the Scrolls', *DSD* 4/3, pp. 265–81.

Collins, J. J. (1997b) *Jewish Wisdom in the Hellenistic Age*, Old Testament Library, Louisville KY: Westminster John Knox Press.

Cowley, A. (1923) *Aramaic Papyri of the Fifth Century BC*, Oxford: Clarendon Press.

Crenshaw, J. L. (1968) 'Amos and the Theophanic Tradition', *ZAW* 80, pp. 203–15.

Crenshaw, J. L. (1974) 'Wisdom' in *Old Testament Form Criticism*, ed. J. H. Hayes, San Antonio: Trinity University Press, pp. 225–64.

Crenshaw, J. L. (1982) *Old Testament Wisdom: An Introduction*, Atlanta: John Knox Press, 1981; London: SCM Press, 1982.

Crenshaw, J. L. (1997) 'The Primacy of Listening in Ben Sira's Pedagogy' in *Wisdom, You Are My Sister: Studies in Honor of Roland E. Murphy, O. Carm., on the Occasion of His Eightieth Birthday*, ed. Michael L. Barré, CBQ Monograph Series 29, Washington DC: Catholic Biblical Association of America.

Crenshaw, J. L. (1998) *Education in Ancient Israel*, New York: Doubleday.

Day, J. (1994) *The Psalms*, Old Testament Guides, Sheffield: Sheffield Academic Press.

Day, J. (1995) 'Foreign Semitic Influence on the Wisdom of Israel and Its Appropriation in the Book of Proverbs' in *Wisdom in Ancient Israel: Essays in Honour of J. A. Emerton*, Cambridge: Cambridge University Press, pp. 55–70.

Dell, K. J. (1991) *The Book of Job as Sceptical Literature*, BZAW 197, Berlin and New York: Walter de Gruyter.

Dell, K. J. (1994a) 'Green Ideas in the Wisdom Tradition', *SJT* 47/4, pp. 423–51.

Dell, K. J. (1994b) 'Ecclesiastes as Wisdom: Consulting Early Interpreters', *VT* 44, pp. 301–29.

Dell, K. J. (1995) 'The Misuse of Forms in Amos', *VT* 45/1, pp. 45–61.

Dell, K. J. (1997) 'On the Development of Wisdom in Israel', *Congress Volume: Cambridge 1995*, SVT 66, ed. J. A. Emerton, Leiden, New York Köln: E. J. Brill, pp. 135–51.

Dell, K. J. (1998) 'The King in the Wisdom Literature' in *King and Messiah in Israel and the Ancient Near East*, ed. J. Day, JSOTS 270, Sheffield: Sheffield Academic Press, pp. 163–86.

Di Lella, A. (1966) 'Conservative and Progressive Theology: Sirach and Wisdom', *CBQ* 28, pp. 139–54.

Di Lella, A. (1995) 'Women in the Wisdom of Ben Sira and the Book of

Judith: A Study in Contrasts and Reversals' in *Congress Volume: Paris, 1992*, ed. J. A. Emerton, SVT 61, Leiden, New York, Köln: E. J. Brill.

Dimant, D. (1993) 'The Qumran Manuscripts: Contents and Significance' in *Time to Prepare a Way in the Wilderness. Papers on the Qumran Scrolls by Fellows of the Institute for Advanced Studies of the Hebrew University, Jerusalem, 1989–1990*, ed. D. Dimant and L. H. Schiffman, Leiden: Brill, pp. 23–49.

Doll, P. (1985) *Menschenschöpfung und Weltschöpfung in der alttestamentlichen Weisheit*, SBS 117, Stuttgart: Katholisches Bibelwork.

Dubarle, A. M. (1946) *Les Sages d'Israël*, Paris: Les Éditions du Cerf.

Elgvin, T., Kister, M., Lim, T., Nitzan, B., Pfann, S., Qimron, E., Shiffman, L. H. and Steudel, A. (1997) *Discoveries in the Judaean Desert XX; Qumran Cave 4. XV, Sapiential Texts, Part 1*, Oxford: Clarendon Press.

Fichtner, J. ([1949] 1976) 'Isaiah among the Wise' in *Studies in Ancient Israelite Wisdom*, ed. J. L. Crenshaw, New York: KTAV.

Fischel, H. A. (1975) 'The Transformation of Wisdom in the World of Midrash' in *Aspects of Wisdom in Judaism and Early Christianity*, ed. R. L. Wilken, Notre Dame and London: University of Notre Dame, pp. 67–101.

Fohrer, G. ([1965] 1970) *Introduction to the Old Testament*, London: SPCK.

Fontaine, C. R. (1982) *Traditional Sayings in the Old Testament*, Sheffield: Almond Press.

Forman, C. C. (1960) 'Koheleth's Use of Genesis', *JSS* 5, pp. 256–63.

Fox, M. V. (1977) 'Frame Narrative and Composition in the Book of Qoheleth', *HUCA* 48, pp. 83–106.

Fox, M. V. (1988) 'The Inner–Structure of Qoheleth's Thought' in *Qoheleth in the Context of Wisdom*, ed. A. Schoors, BETL 136, Leuven: Leuven University Press, pp. 158–78.

Fredericks, D. C. (1988) *Qohelet's Language: Re–evaluating Its Nature and Date*, Lewiston, Queenston: Mellon.

Gemser, B. (1975) 'The Spiritual Structure of Biblical Aphoristic Wisdom' in *Studies in Ancient Israelite Wisdom*, ed. J. L. Crenshaw, New York: KTAV, pp. 208–19.

Gerstenberger, E. (1962) 'The Woe-Oracles of the Prophets', *JBL* 81, pp. 249–63.

Gerstenberger, E. (1974) 'Psalms' in *Old Testament Form Criticism*, ed. J. H. Hayes, San Antonio: Trinity University Press, pp. 179–221.

Gerstenberger, E. (1991) *Psalms, Part 1 with an Introduction to Cultic Poetry*, The Forms of the Old Testament Literature Volume XIV, ed. R. Knierim and G. M. Tucker, Grand Rapids MI: Eerdmans.

Gilbert, M. (1984) 'Wisdom Literature' in *Jewish Writings of the Second Temple Period*, ed. M. Stone, CRINT 2/2, Philadelphia: Fortress Press, pp. 283–324.

Goldingay, J. (1989) *Daniel*, Word Biblical Commentary 30, Dallas TX: Word Books.

Golka, F. (1993) *The Leopard's Spots: Biblical and African Wisdom in Proverbs*, Edinburgh: T & T Clark.

Good, E. M. (1965) *Irony in the Old Testament*, London: SPCK, pp. 168–95.

Good, E. M. (1990) *In Turns of Tempest: A Reading of Job with a Translation*, Stanford, CA: Stanford University Press.

Goodrick, A. T. S. (1913) *The Book of Wisdom*, London: Rivingtons.

Gordis, R. (1962) *Koheleth, The Man and his World*, New York: Bloch Publishing.

Gordis, R. (1939–40) 'Quotations in Wisdom Literature', *JQR* NS 30, pp. 123–47; reprinted in *Poets, Prophets, Sages*, Bloomington and London: Indiana University Press, 1971, pp. 160–97.

Gordon, E. I. (1959) *Sumerian Proverbs. Glimpses of Everyday Life in Ancient Mesopotamia*, Philadelphia: University Museum, University of Pennsylvania.

Grabbe, L. L. (1997) *Wisdom of Solomon*, Guides to Apocrypha and Pseudepigrapha, Sheffield: Sheffield Academic Press.

Greenfield, J. C. (1995) 'The Wisdom of Ahiqar' in *Wisdom in Ancient Israel: Essays in Honour of J. A. Emerton*, Cambridge: Cambridge University Press, pp. 43–54.

Gutiérrez, G. (1987) *On Job*, Maryknoll NY: Orbis Books.

Habel, N. C. (1985) *The Book of Job*, Old Testament Library, London: SCM Press; Philadelphia: Westminster Press.

Harrington, D. J. (1980) 'The Wisdom of the Scribe According to Ben Sira' in *Ideal Figures in Ancient Judaism: Profiles and Paradigms*, ed. G. W. E. Nickelsburg and J. J. Collins, SBL Septuagint and Cognate Studies 12, Chico, CA: Scholars Press, pp. 181–8.

Harrington, D. J. (1996a) *Wisdom Texts from Qumran*, London and New York: Routledge.

Harrington, D. J. (1996b) 'The Raz Nihyeh in a Qumran Wisdom Text (1Q26, 4Q415–418, 423)', *Revue de Qumran* 17, pp. 549–53.

Harrington, D. J. (1997) 'Two Early Jewish Approaches to Wisdom, Sirach and Qumran Sapiential Work A', *JSOP* 16, pp. 25–38.

Harvey, J. D. (1993) 'Toward a Degree of Order in Ben Sira's Book', *ZAW* 105, pp. 52–62.

Haspecker, J. (1967) *Gottesfurcht bei Jesus Sirach*, Analecta Biblica 30, Rome: Biblical Institute Press.

Heaton, E. W. (1974) *Solomon's New Men*, London and New York: Pica Press.

Heaton, E. W. (1994) *The School Tradition in the Old Testament*, Oxford: Oxford University Press.

Heinisch, P. (1908) *Die Griechische Philosophie im Buche der Weisheit*, Alttestamentliche Abhandlungen 1, Münster i. W.: Aschendorffsche Verlagsbuchhandlung.

Hengel, M. ([1973] 1974) *Judaism and Hellenism*, London: SCM Press.

Hoffman, Y. (1981) 'The Relation between the Prologue and the Speech-Cycles in Job', *VT* 31, pp. 160–70.

Horst, P. W. van der (1978) *The Sentences of Pseudo-Phocylides*, Leiden: Brill.

Horst, P. W. van der (1988) 'Pseudo-Phocylides Revisited' in *JSOP* 3, pp. 3–30;

reprinted in *Essays on the Jewish World of Early Christianity*, Göttingen: Vandenhoeck & Ruprecht, 1990, pp. 35–62.

Humphreys, W. L. (1978) 'The Motif of the Wise Courtier in the Book of Proverbs' in *Israelite Wisdom*, ed. J. G. Gammie et al., Missoula, MT: Scholars Press, pp. 177–90.

Jensen, J. (1973) *The Use of tôrâ by Isaiah. His Debate with the Wisdom Tradition*, Washington DC: Catholic Biblical Association of America.

Johnston, R. K. (1976) ' "Confessions of a Workaholic": A Reappraisal of Qoheleth', *CBQ* 38, pp. 14–28.

Jung, C. G. ([1952] 1954) *Answer to Job*, London: Routledge and Kegan Paul.

Kayatz, C. (1966) *Studien zur Proverbien 1–9*, WMANT 22, Neukirchen-Vluyn: Neukirchener Verlag.

Kenworthy, A. W. (1974) 'The Nature and Authority of Old Testament Wisdom Family Ethics, with Special Reference to Proverbs and Sirach', dissertation, University of Melbourne.

Kieweler, V. (1992) *Ben Sira zwischen Judentum und Hellenismus. Eine Auseinandersetzung mit Th. Middendorp*, Beitrage zur Erforschung des Alten Testament und des antiken Judentums 30, Frankfurt: Peter Lang.

Kloppenburg, J. S. (1982) 'Isis and Sophia in the Book of Wisdom', *Harvard Theological Review* 75, pp. 57–84.

Kolarcik, M. (1991) *The Ambiguity of Death in the Book of Wisdom 1—6: A Study of Literary Structure and Interpretation*, Analecta Biblica 127, Rome: Biblical Institute Press.

Kramer, S. N. (1958) *History Begins at Sumer*, London: Thames and Hudson.

Kramer, S. N. (1967) *The Sumerians: Their History, Culture and Character*, Chicago: University of Chicago Press, 3rd edn.

Kselman, J. S. (1997) 'Psalm 36' in *Wisdom, You Are My Sister: Studies in Honor of Roland E. Murphy, O. Carm., on the Occasion of His Eightieth Birthday*, ed. M. L. Barré, CBQ Monograph Series 29, Washington: Catholic Biblical Association of America.

Kuntz, J. K. (1974) 'The Canonical Wisdom Psalms of Ancient Israel, Their Rhetorical, Thematic and Formal Dimensions', *Rhetorical Criticism: Essays in Honor of James Muilenburg*, PTMS 1, ed. J. J. Jackson et al., Pittsburgh: Pickwick, pp.186–222.

Lambert, W. G. (1960) *Babylonian Wisdom Literature*, Oxford: Oxford University Press.

Lang, B. (1975) *Frau Weisheit, Deutung einer biblischen Gestalt*, Düsseldorf: Patmos-Verlag.

Larcher, C. (1983–5) *Le Livre de la Sagesse ou la Sagesse de Salomon* (3 vols), Études Bibliques Nouvelle Série 1, Paris: Gabalda.

Leeuwen, R. C. van (1997) 'Scribal Wisdom and a Biblical Proverb at Qumran', *DSD* 4/3, pp. 255–64.

Lemaire, A. (1981) *Les écoles et la formation de la Bible dans l'ancien Israël*, OBO 39, Fribourg: Éditions Universitaires; Göttingen: Vandenhoeck & Ruprecht.

Lévêque, J. (1974) 'Le contrepoint théologique apporté par la reflexion sapientielle' in *Questions Disputées de l'Ancien Testament*, ed. C. Brekelmans, Louvain: Leuven University Press, and Peeters, pp. 183–202.

Levine, E. (1997) 'The Humor in Qoheleth', *ZAW* 109, pp. 71–83.

Lichtheim, M. (1983) *Late Egyptian Wisdom Literature in the International Context: A Study of Demotic Instructions*, OBO 52, Fribourg: Éditions Universitaires; Göttingen: Vandenhoeck & Ruprecht.

Lindblom, J. (1955) 'Wisdom in the Old Testament Prophets', SVT 3, pp. 192–204.

Loader, J. A. (1979) *Polar Structures in the Book of Qoheleth*, BZAW 152, Berlin and New York: Walter de Gruyter.

Lowndes Lipscomb, W. and Sanders, J. A. (1978) 'Wisdom at Qumran' in *Israelite Wisdom: Theological and Literary Essays in Honor of Samuel Terrien*, ed. J. G. Gammie et al., Missoula, MT: Scholars Press, pp. 277–85.

Luther, M. ([1536] 1972) 'Notes on Ecclesiastes', *Luther's Works* 15, St Louis: Concordia Publishing House, pp. 3–187.

Macintosh, A. A. (1995) 'Hosea and the Wisdom Tradition: Dependence and Independence' in *Wisdom in Ancient Israel: Essays in Honour of J. A. Emerton*, ed. J. Day, R. P. Gordon and H. G. M. Williamson, Cambridge: Cambridge University Press, pp. 124–32.

Mack, B. L. (1973) *Logos und Sophia: Untersuchungen zur Weisheitstheologie im hellenistischen Judentum*, SUNT 10, Göttingen: Vandenhoeck & Ruprecht.

Mack, B. L. (1985) *Wisdom and the Hebrew Epic: Ben Sira's Hymn in Praise of the Fathers, Chicago Studies in the History of Judaism*, Chicago: University of Chicago Press.

Mack-Fisher, L. (1990) 'The Scribe (and Sage) in the Royal Court at Ugarit' in *The Sage in Israel and in the Ancient Near East*, ed. J. G. Gammie and L. G. Perdue, Winona Lake: Eisenbrauns, pp. 109–16.

Manson, T. W. (1957) *The Sayings of Jesus*, London: SCM Press.

Marshall, J. T. (1905) *Job and His Comforters*, London: James Clarke and Co.

McKane, W. (1965) *Prophets and Wise Men*, SBT 44, London: SCM Press.

McKane, W. (1970) *Proverbs. A New Approach*, Old Testament Library, London: SCM Press.

McKenzie, J. L. (1967) 'Reflections on Wisdom', *JBL* 86, pp. 1–9.

Middendorp, T. (1973) *Die Stellung Jesu Ben Siras zwischen Judentum und Hellenismus*, Leiden: Brill.

Moore, R. D. (1979–81) 'Personification of the Seduction of Evil. The Wiles of the Wicked Woman', *Revue de Qumran* 10, pp. 505–19.

Morgan, D. F. (1981) *Wisdom in the Old Testament Traditions*, Atlanta: John Knox Press.

Mowinckel, S. (1955) 'Psalms and Wisdom', SVT 3, pp. 205–44.

Murphy, R. E. (1992) *Ecclesiastes*, Word Biblical Commentary, Dallas TX: Word Books.

Murray, R. (1992) *The Cosmic Covenant: Biblical Themes of Justice, Peace and the Integrity of Creation*, Heythrop Monographs 7, London: Sheed and Ward.

Newsom, C. (1990) ' "Sectually Explicit" Literature from Qumran', *The Hebrew Bible and Its Interpreters*, ed. W. H. Propp, B. Halpern and D. N. Freedman, Biblical and Judaic Studies 1, Winona Lake IN: Eisenbrauns, pp. 167–87.

Nougayrol, J. (1952) 'Une version ancienne du "juste souffrant" ', *RB* 59, pp. 239–50.

Oesterley, W. O. E. and Box, G. H. (1911) *The Religion and Worship of the Synagogue*, London: Sir Isaac Pitman and Sons Ltd., 2nd edn.

Perdue, L. G. (1977) *Wisdom and Cult*, SBL Dissertation Series 30, Missoula, MT: Scholars Press.

Perdue, L. G. (1986) 'The Wisdom Sayings of Jesus', *A Journal of the Foundations and Facets of Western Culture* 2/3, pp. 3–35.

Perdue, L. G. (1991) *Wisdom in Revolt*, Sheffield: Almond Press.

Perdue, L. G. (1994) *Wisdom and Creation*, Nashville: Abingdon Press.

Perry, T. A. (1993) *Dialogues with Qoheleth: The Book of Ecclesiastes: Translation and Commentary*, University Park: Pennsylvania State University Press.

Preuss, H. D. ([1991] 1995–6) *Old Testament Theology*, Louisville, KY: Westminster John Knox Press; Edinburgh: T & T Clark.

Pritchard, J. B. (1969) *Ancient Near Eastern Texts Relating to the Old Testament*, Princeton, NJ: Princeton University Press, 3rd edn.

Purinton, C. E. (1928) 'Translation Greek in the Wisdom of Solomon', *JBL* 47, pp. 276–304.

Rad, G. von ([1958–61] 1962a) *Old Testament Theology*, Volume 1, Edinburgh and London: Oliver and Boyd, 1962; SCM Press, 1975.

Rad, G. von ([1958–61] 1962b) *Old Testament Theology*, Volume 2, Edinburgh: Oliver and Boyd, 1962; SCM Press, 1975.

Rad, G. von ([1944] 1966a) 'The Beginning of Historical Writing in Ancient Israel' in *The Problem of the Hexateuch and Other Essays*, Edinburgh and London: Oliver and Boyd, 1966; London: SCM Press, 1984, pp. 166–204.

Rad, G. von ([1953] 1966b) 'Some Aspects of the Old Testament World View' in *The Problem of the Hexateuch and Other Essays*, Edinburgh and London: Oliver and Boyd, 1966; London: SCM Press, 1984, pp. 144–65.

Rad, G. von ([1953] 1966c) 'The Joseph Narrative and Ancient Wisdom' in *The Problem of the Hexateuch and Other Essays*, Edinburgh and London: Oliver and Boyd, 1966; London: SCM Press, 1984, pp. 292–300.

Rad, G. von ([1970] 1972) *Wisdom in Israel*, London: SCM Press.

Ranston, H. (1930) *The Old Testament Wisdom Books and Their Teaching*, London: Epworth Press.

Reese, J. M. (1970) *Hellenistic Influence on the Book of Wisdom and Its Consequences*, Analecta Biblica 41, Rome: Biblical Institute Press.

Richter, W. (1966) *Recht und Ethos: Versuch einer Ortung des Weisheitlichen Mahnspruches*, München: Kösel Verlag.

Ringgren, H. (1947) *Word and Wisdom. Studies in the Hypostatization of Divine Qualities and Functions in the Ancient Near East*, Lund: Ohlssons.

Roth, W. (1980) 'On the Gnomic Discursive Wisdom of Jesus Ben Sira', *Semeia* 17, pp. 59–79.

Rowley, H. H. (1970) *Job*, New Century Bible, London: Thomas Nelson and Sons.

Sanders, J. T. (1983) *Ben Sira and Demotic Wisdom*, SBL MS 28, Chico CA: Scholars Press.

Sawyer, J. F. A. (1982) 'Was Jeshua Ben Sira a Priest?' *Proceedings of the Eighth World Congress of Jewish Studies, Jerusalem, August 16–21, 1981*, World Union of Jewish Studies, Jerusalem.

Schlobin, R. C. (1992) 'Prototypic Horror: The Genre of the Book of Job', *Semeia* 60, pp. 23–38.

Schmid, H. H. (1966) *Wesen und Geschichte der Weisheit*, BZAW 101, Berlin: Töpelmann.

Schmid, H. H. (1984) 'Creation, Righteousness, and Salvation: "Creation Theology" as the Broad Horizon of Biblical Theology' in *Creation in the Old Testament*, ed. B. W. Anderson, London: SCM Press; Philadelphia: Fortress Press, pp. 102–117.

Schnabel, E. J. (1985), *Law and Wisdom from Ben Sira to Paul: A Tradition-Historical Enquiry into the Relation of Law, Wisdom and Ethics*, WUNT 2.16, Tübingen: JCB Mohr (Paul Siebeck).

Schoedel, W. R. (1975) 'Jewish Wisdom and the Formation of the Christian Ascetic' in *Aspects of Wisdom in Judaism and Early Christianity*, ed. R. L. Wilken, Notre Dame: University of Notre Dame Press, pp. 169–99.

Scott, B. B. (1990) 'Jesus as Sage: An Innovating Voice in Common Wisdom' in *The Sage in Israel and the Ancient Near East*, ed. J. G. Gammie and L. G. Perdue, Winona Lake: Eisenbrauns, pp. 319–416.

Scott, R. B. Y. (1955) 'Solomon and the Beginnings of Wisdom in Israel', SVT 3, pp. 262–79.

Sellin, E. ([1910] 1923) *Introduction to the Old Testament*, London: Hodder and Stoughton.

Seow, C. L. (1997) *Ecclesiastes*, Anchor Bible, New York: Doubleday.

Shead, A. (1996) 'Ecclesiastes from the outside in', *Revue Théologiques et Réligieuses* 55, pp. 24–37.

Skehan, P. W. and Di Lella, A. (1987) *The Wisdom of Ben Sira*, Anchor Bible 39, New York: Doubleday.

Smith, J. Z. (1975) 'Wisdom and Apocalyptic', *Religious Syncretism in Antiquity: Essays in Conversation with G. Widengren*, ed. B. A. Pearson, Missoula, MT: Scholars Press, pp. 131–56.

Snaith, J. C. (1975) 'Ben Sira's Supposed Love of Liturgy', *VT* 25, pp. 167–74.

Snaith, N. (1968) *The Book of Job: Its Origin and Purpose*, London: SCM Press.

Stadelmann, H. (1980) *Ben Sira als Schriftgelehrter. Eine Untersuchung zum Berufsbild des vormakkabäischen Sofer unter Berücksichtigung eines Ver-*

hältnisses zu Priester – Propheten – und Weisheitslehrertum, WUNT 2/6, Tübingen: JCB Mohr (Paul Siebeck).

Steck, O. H. (1980) 'Bemerkungen zur thematischen Einheit von Psalm 19, 2–7' in *Werden und Wirken des Alten Testaments: Festschrift für Claus Westermann zum 70. Geburtstag*, ed. R. Albertz et al., Göttingen: Vandenhoeck & Ruprecht; Neukirchen–Vluyn: Neukirchener Verlag, pp. 318–24.

Steiner, G. (1979) 'Tragedy; Remorse and Justice', *The Listener* 102, pp. 508–11.

Stuckenbruck, L. (1999) 'Wisdom and Holiness at Qumran: Strategies for Dealing with Sin in the *Community Rule*' in *Where Shall Wisdom Be Found? Wisdom in the Bible, the Church and the Contemporary World*, ed. S. C. Barton, Edinburgh: T & T Clark, pp. 47–60.

Terrien, S. (1996) *The Iconography of Job through the Centuries. Artists as Biblical Interpreters*, University Park: Pennsylvania State University Press.

Trenchard, W. C. (1982) *Ben Sira's View of Women*, Brown Judaic Studies, Chico CA: Scholars Press.

VanderKam, J. C. (1997) 'Mantic Wisdom in the Dead Sea Scrolls', *DSD* 4/3, pp. 336–53.

Vogels, W. (1995) *Job, homme qui a bien parlé de Dieu*, Paris: Éditions du Cerf.

Walsh, J. T. (1982) 'Despair as a Theological Virtue in the Spirituality of Ecclesiastes', *Biblical Theology Bulletin* 12, pp. 46–9.

Weeks, S. (1994) *Early Israelite Wisdom*, Oxford: Oxford University Press.

Weinfeld, M. (1972) *Deuteronomy and the Deuteronomic School*, Oxford: Oxford University Press.

Westermann, C. ([1956] 1981) *The Structure of the Book of Job*, Philadelphia: Fortress Press.

Westermann, C. ([1968] 1978) *Blessing in the Bible and the Life of the Church*, Philadelphia: Fortress Press.

Westermann, C. ([1990] 1995) *Roots of Wisdom*, Göttingen: Vandenhoeck & Ruprecht; Edinburgh: T & T Clark.

Whedbee, J. W. (1971) *Isaiah and Wisdom*, New York: Abington Press.

Whedbee, J. W. (1977) 'The Comedy of Job', *Semeia* 7 (Studies in the Book of Job), ed. R. Polzin and D. Robertson, Missoula: Scholars Press, pp. 1–39.

Whitley, C. F. (1979) *Koheleth: His Language and Thought*, BZAW 148, Berlin: Walter de Gruyter.

Whybray, R. N. (1965) *Wisdom in Proverbs: The Concept of Wisdom in Proverbs 1—9*, SBT 45, London: SCM Press.

Whybray, R. N. (1968) *The Succession Narrative*, SBT Second Series 9, London: SCM Press.

Whybray, R. N. (1974) *The Intellectual Tradition in the Old Testament*, BZAW 135, Berlin and New York: Walter de Gruyter.

Whybray, R. N. (1981) 'The Identification and Use of Quotations in Ecclesiastes', *Congress Volume: Vienna, 1980*, ed. J. A. Emerton, SVT 32, pp. 435–51.

Whybray, R. N. (1982) 'Qoheleth, Preacher of Joy?', *JSOT* 23, pp. 87–98.

Whybray, R. N. (1990) *Wealth and Poverty in the Book of Proverbs*, Sheffield: JSOT Press.

Whybray, R. N. (1994a) *The Composition of the Book of Proverbs*, Sheffield: JSOT Press.

Whybray, R. N. (1994b) 'The Structure and Composition of Proverbs 22:17— 24:22' in *Crossing the Boundaries: Essays in Biblical Interpretation in Honour of Michael D. Goulder*, ed. S. E. Porter, P. Joyce and D. E. Orton, Leiden: Brill, pp. 83–96.

Whybray, R. N. (1994c) *Proverbs*, New Century Bible Commentary, London: Marshall Pickering; Grand Rapids MI: Eerdmans.

Whybray, R. N. (1995) 'The Wisdom Psalms' in *Wisdom in Ancient Israel: Essays in honour of J. A. Emerton*, ed. J. Day, R. P. Gordon and H. G. M. Williamson, Cambridge: Cambridge University Press, pp. 152–60.

Whybray, R. N. (1996) *Reading the Psalms as a Book*, Sheffield: Sheffield Academic Press.

Wilken, R. L. (1975) 'Wisdom and Philosophy in Early Christianity' in *Aspects of Wisdom in Judaism and Early Christianity*, ed. R. L. Wilken, Notre Dame: University of Notre Dame Press, pp. 143–68.

Williams, D. S. (1994) 'The Date of Ecclesiasticus', *VT* 44, pp. 563–65.

Williams, R. J. (1972) 'Scribal Training in Ancient Egypt', *JAOS* 92/2, pp. 214–21.

Williamson, H. G. M. (1995) 'Isaiah and the Wise' in *Wisdom in Ancient Israel: Essays in Honour of J. A. Emerton*, ed. J. Day, R. P. Gordon and H. G. M. Williamson, Cambridge: Cambridge University Press, pp. 133–41.

Winston, D. (1979) *The Wisdom of Solomon*, Garden City: Doubleday.

Winston, D. (1989) 'Theodicy in Ben Sira and Stoic Philosophy' in *Of Scholars, Savants, and their Texts: Studies in Philosophy and Religious Thought. Essays in Honour of Arthur Hyman*, ed. R. Link-Salinger et al., New York: Peter Lang, pp. 239–49.

Witherington III, B. (1994) *Jesus the Sage: The Pilgrimage of Wisdom*, Edinburgh: T & T Clark.

Wolde, E. van (1997) *Mr and Mrs Job*, London: SCM Press.

Wolfers, D. (1995) *Deep Things Out of Darkness: The Book of Job, Essays and a New English Translation*, Grand Rapids MI: Eerdmans.

Wolff, H. W. ([1961] 1974) *Hosea*, Hermeneia, Philadelphia: Fortress Press.

Wolff, H. W. ([1964] 1973) *Amos the Prophet: The Man and His Background*, Philadelphia: Fortress Press.

Wolff, H. W. ([1975] 1977) *Joel and Amos*, Hermeneia, Philadelphia: Fortress Press.

Wolff, H. W. ([1978] 1981) *Micah the Prophet*, Philadelphia: Fortress Press.

Woude, A. S. van der (1995) 'Wisdom at Qumran' in *Wisdom in Ancient Israel: Essays in Honour of J. A. Emerton*, ed. J. Day, R. P. Gordon and H. G. M. Williamson, Cambridge: Cambridge University Press, pp. 244–56.

Wright, A. G. (1967) 'The Structure of the Book of Wisdom', *Biblica* 48, pp. 165–84.

Zimmerli, W. (1980) *Das Buch des Predigers Salomo*, Das Alte Testament Deutsch, Göttingen: Vandenhoeck & Ruprecht, 3rd edn.

Zimmerman, F. (1966–7) 'The Book of Wisdom: Its Language and Character', *JQR* NS 57, pp. 1–27, 101–35.

Zuckerman, B. (1991) *Job the Silent: A Study of Historical Counterpoint*, Oxford: Oxford University Press.

BIBLE REFERENCES

INDEX OF AUTHORS

SUBJECT INDEX